A Lost Language and Other Essays on Chaucer

A Lost Language
and Other Essays on Chaucer

by

SISTER M. MADELEVA, C.S.C.

SHEED AND WARD
NEW YORK
1951

NIHIL OBSTAT
Philip J. Donnelly, S. J.
Censor Deputatus

IMPRIMATUR
✠ Richard J. Cushing
Archbishop of Boston

Boston, January 30, 1951

This "litel bok" is

for

Mother M. Rose Elizabeth, C.S.C.

Acknowledgments

CHAUCER'S NUNS was originally published as the title essay in a volume of critical literary studies.

A LOST LANGUAGE is reprinted from *Thought* with the kind permission of the editors.

Houghton-Mifflin Company has kindly authorized the use of the quotations from the Chaucer text.

Author's Note

THE BARRIER of language stands today between Chaucer and most of his possible readers. Many of our best studies of him constitute almost as much of a barrier. They are scholarly beyond the competence of those who would like to know our first and greatest narrative poet in his inimitable humanity without Middle English and the idiom of research.

These brief essays have attempted to provide some such reading knowledge of parts of Chaucer. They are not entirely beyond the pale of scholarly preparation. Most of them were written in Chaucer's own Oxford. But they make no attempt at research methods or ends. Indeed, they add no cubit to the stature of Chaucer on these terms.

They are conscious of a simple, lovable, elfish man, albeit a genius, writing out of the sheer impact of his own abounding gift, for folk not unlike himself, not unlike you and me. Some aspects of these common likenesses they have tried to set down.

As prefatory to each of the first five essays the appropriate text from Chaucer may be used.

These texts have been selected from the Cambridge Edition of

The Poetical Works of Chaucer, edited by
F. N. Robinson
Houghton Mifflin Company, Boston

S.M.M.

Contents

Contents

A Lost Language

An A B C

ALMIGHTY and al merciable queene,
To whom that al this world fleeth for socour,
To have relees of sinne, of sorwe, and teene,
Glorious virgine, of alle floures flour,
To thee I flee, confounded in errour.
Help and releeve, thou mighti debonayre,
Have mercy on my perilous langour!
Venquisshed me hath my cruel adversaire.

Bountee so fix hath in thin herte his tente,
That wel I wot thou wolt my socour bee;
Thou canst not warne him that with good entente
Axeth thin helpe, thin herte is ay so free.
Thou art largesse of pleyn felicitee,
Haven of refut, of quiete, and of reste.
Loo, how that theeves sevene chasen mee!
Help, lady bright, er that my ship to-breste!

Comfort is noon but in yow, ladi deere;
For, loo, my sinne and my confusioun,
Which oughten not in thi presence appeere,
Han take on me a greevous accioun
Of verrey right and desperacioun;
And, as bi right, thei mighten wel susteene

3

That I were wurthi my dampnacioun,
Nere merci of you, blisful hevene queene!

Dowte is ther noon, thou queen of misericorde,
That thou n'art cause of grace and merci heere;
God vouched sauf thurgh thee with us to accorde.
For, certes, Crystes blisful mooder deere,
Were now the bowe bent in swich maneere
As it was first, of justice and of ire,
The rightful God nolde of no mercy heere;
But thurgh thee han we grace, as we desire.

Evere hath myn hope of refut been in thee,
For heer-biforn ful ofte, in many a wyse,
Hast thou to misericorde receyved me.
But merci, ladi, at the grete assyse,
Whan we shule come bifore the hye justyse!
So litel fruit shal thanne in me be founde
That, but thou er that day me wel chastyse,
Of verrey right my werk wol me confounde.

Fleeinge, I flee for socour to thi tente
Me for to hide from tempeste ful of dreede,
Biseeching yow that ye you not absente,
Thouh I be wikke. O help yit at this neede!
Al have I ben a beste in wil and deede,
Yit, ladi, thou me clothe with thi grace.
Thin encmy and myn—ladi, tak heede!—
Unto my deth in poynt is me to chace!

Glorious mayde and mooder, which that nevere
Were bitter, neither in erthe nor in see,
But ful of swetnesse and of merci evere,
Help that my Fader be not wroth with me.
Spek thou, for I ne dar not him ysee,
So have I doon in erthe, allas the while!
That certes, but if thou my socour bee,
To stink eterne he wole my gost exile.

He vouched sauf, tel him, as was his wille,
Bicome a man, to have oure alliaunce,
And with his precious blood he wrot the bille
Upon the crois, as general acquitaunce,
To every penitent in ful creaunce;
And therfore, ladi bright, thou for us praye.
Thanne shalt thou bothe stinte al his grevaunce,
And make oure foo to failen of his praye.

I wot it wel, thou wolt ben oure socour,
Thou art so ful of bowntee, in certeyn.
For, whan a soule falleth in errour,
Thi pitee goth and haleth him ayein.
Thanne makest thou his pees with his sovereyn,
And bringest him out of the crooked strete.
Whoso thee loveth, he shal not love in veyn;
That shal he fynde, as he the lyf shal lete.

Kalenderes enlumyned ben thei
That in this world ben lighted with thi name;

And whoso goth to yow the righte wey,
Him thar not drede in soule to be lame.
Now, queen of comfort, sith thou art that same
To whom I seeche for my medicyne,
Lat not my foo no more my wounde entame;
Myn hele into thin hand al I resygne.

Ladi, thi sorwe kan I not portreye
Under the cros, ne his greevous penaunce.
But for youre bothes peynes I yow preye,
Lat not oure alder foo make his bobaunce
That he hath in his lystes of mischaunce
Convict that ye bothe have bought so deere.
As I seide erst, thou ground of oure substaunce,
Continue on us thi pitous eyen cleere!

Moises, that saugh the bush with flawmes rede
Brenninge, of which ther never a stikke brende,
Was signe of thin unwemmed maidenhede.
Thou art the bush on which ther gan descende
The Holi Gost, the which that Moyses wende
Had ben a-fyr; and this was in figure.
Now, ladi, from the fyr thou us defende
Which that in helle eternalli shal dure.

Noble princesse, that nevere haddest peere,
Certes, if any comfort in us bee,
That cometh of thee, thou Cristes mooder deere.

We han noon oother melodye or glee
Us to rejoyse in oure adversitee,
Ne advocat noon that wole and dar so preye
For us, and that for litel hire as yee,
That helpen for an Ave-Marie or tweye.

O verrey light of eyen that ben blynde,
O verrey lust of labour and distresse,
O tresoreere of bountee to mankynde,
Thee whom God ches to mooder for humblesse!
From his ancille he made the maistresse
Of hevene and erthe, oure bille up for to beede.
This world awaiteth evere on thi goodnesse,
For thou ne failest nevere wight at neede.

Purpos I have sum time for to enquere
Wherfore and whi the Holi Gost thee soughte,
Whan Gabrielles vois cam to thin ere.
He not to werre us swich a wonder wroughte,
But for to save us that he sithen boughte;
Thanne needeth us no wepen us for to save,
But oonly ther we dide not, as us oughte,
Doo penitence, and merci axe and have.

Queen of comfort, yit whan I me bithinke
That I agilt have bothe him and thee,
And that my soule is worthi for to sinke,
Allas! I caityf, whider may I flee?

Who shal unto thi Sone my mene bee?
Who, but thiself, that art of pitee welle?
Thou hast more reuthe on oure adversitee
Than in this world might any tonge telle.

Redresse me, mooder, and me chastise,
For certeynly my Faderes chastisinge,
That dar I nouht abiden in no wise,
So hidous is his rightful rekenynge.
Mooder, of whom oure merci gan to springe,
Beth ye my juge and eek my soules leche;
For evere in you is pitee haboundinge
To ech that wole of pitee you biseeche.

Soth is that God ne granteth no pitee
Withoute thee; for God, of his goodnesse,
Foryiveth noon, but it like unto thee.
He hath thee maked vicaire and maistresse
Of al this world, and eek governouresse
Of hevene, and he represseth his justise
After thi wil; and therfore in witnesse
He hath thee corowned in so rial wise.

Temple devout, ther God hath his woninge,
Fro which these misbileeved deprived been,
To you my soule penitent I bringe.
Receyve me—I can no ferther fleen!
With thornes venymous, O hevene queen,

For which the eerthe acursed was ful yore,
I am so wounded, as ye may wel seen,
That I am lost almost, it smert so sore.

Virgine, that are so noble of apparaile,
And ledest us into the hye tour
Of Paradys, thou me wisse and counsaile
How I may have thi grace and thi socour,
All have I ben in filthe and in errour.
Ladi, unto that court thou me ajourne
That cleped is thi bench, O freshe flour!
Ther as that merci evere shal sojourne.

Xristus, thi sone, that in this world alighte
Upon the cros to suffre his passioun,
And eek that Longius his herte pighte,
And made his herte blood to renne adoun,
And al was this for my salvacioun;
And I to him am fals and eek unkynde,
And yit he wole not my dampnacioun—
This thanke I yow, socour of al mankynde!

Ysaac was figure of his deth, certeyn,
That so fer forth his fader wolde obeye
That him ne roughte nothing to be slayn;
Right soo thi Sone list, as a lamb, to deye.
Now, ladi ful of merci, I yow preye,
Sith he his merci mesured so large,

Be ye not skant; for alle we singe and seye
That ye ben from vengeaunce ay oure targe.

Zacharie yow clepeth the open welle
To wasshe sinful soule out of his gilt.
Therfore this lessoun oughte I wel to telle,
That, nere thi tender herte, we were spilt.
Now, ladi bryghte, sith thou canst and wilt
Ben to the seed of Adam merciable,
Bring us to that palais that is bilt
To penitentes that ben to merci able.

Amen.

EXPLICIT CARMEN.

A Lost Language

Perhaps at the age of nineteen, perhaps at the age of twenty-nine, or in the years between, Chaucer wrote in twenty-six eight-line stanzas beginning with successive letters of the alphabet the poem known as *An A B C*. Rather, he made in this form a free translation of a French original verse prayer to Our Lady. Ordinarily it is dismissed as uninteresting because it is immature, as unimportant because it is a translation. Yet there are those who care for the poems of the young Chaucer quite as much as the poems of the young Milton, and his first translations can have at least the same interest as those of Chapman. There are those who care for the *A B C* because it is his first printed prayer and the only one remaining to us of the beautiful poems to the Blessed Virgin Mary for which his admirer, Lydgate, gave him such specific praise. In this little study of Chaucer's prayers, it is obviously the one with which to begin.

The first thing that he did with his original was to expand the octo- into a decasyllabic line. This, of course, he did as a poet and not as a translator. The next thing that he did was to transform a devout convention into a divine conversation with his "almighty and al merciable queene," to sing rather than to say his prayer. Whatever the French lost in translation, it did not lose its life. It is beautiful to listen to this singing lad, this Chaucer, vacillating between doctrinal desolation in himself and doctrinal delight in his Lady with the abashed ardor of a boy and the conversational ease that is the ideal but rarely the achievement of written prayer. For conversation is the manner of the poem and doctrine is its matter, the doctrine of devotion to the Mother of God.

That devotion, always in the heart of the Church, was conspicuously on her lips in the liturgy, in the works of her children, in the lives of her saints during those three centuries of which Chaucer's is central. Three great feasts to honor her, the Nativity, the Annunciation, the Presentation, two great religious orders to serve humanity through her, the Carmelites and the Servites of Mary, were all established less than a hundred years before Chaucer was born. Already the firebrand of St. Dominic and the honeyed prayers of St. Bernard were light and sweetness to a world in love with Mary. Chaucer, in writing of her, was living the devotional life of his time. This first poem of his is a composite of the central doctrines, titles and devotions under which the Church honors her: "almighty and al merciable queene," "glorious virgine," "Crystes blisful mooder deere." In these are implied her power to help, her purity to inspire, her tenderness to suffer with and save the sinner. The mediaeval world, whatever else it did, prostrated itself in contrition before the Refuge of sinners. Chaucer was in that kneeling world.

His business with Mary is pardon and praise; pardon in that his need is so dire, praise because her meed is absolute. A side note in an early manuscript describes the situation thus: "Chaucer Deuotissima oracio (ad) Mariam, pro omni tentacione tribulacione necessitate angustia." He puts the matter on a definitely conversational basis, on a plane just one degree below the Godhead. It is delightful to observe him there, so young and so impulsively at ease. He uses to this "noble princesse, that nevere haddest peere" three idioms: the soldier's, the merchant's, the lawyer's. The young squire it is, in desperation, who speaks:

> Thin enemy and myn—ladi, tak heede!—
> Unto my deth in poynt is me to chace.

As a boy's predicament the situation is tremendously human and vivid; as a prayer, in all its humorous nervousness, it is superlative. Recovering courage and getting down to the business possibilities of Christ's pardon, he speaks the language of his father's house:

> He vouched sauf, tel him, as was his wille,
> Bicome a man, to have oure alliaunce,

And with his precious blood he wrot the bille
Upon the crois, as general acquitaunce.

Never did the idiom of business fit more patly into a young man's prayers. But his last appeal is in terms more technical and probably more recently acquired: Having described his case in terms of supreme understatement he makes his brave legal gesture:

Ladi, unto that court thou me ajourne
That cleped is thi bench, O freshe flour!
Ther as that merci evere shal sojourne.

One likes to think that perhaps during hours between lessons at the Temple he did this pretty, boyish bit of special pleading.

Nothing but youth and the rigidity of the alphabet can explain the glorious camaraderie with divinity of this:

Purpos I have sum time for to enquere
Wherfore and whi the Holi Gost thee soughte.
Whan Gabrielles vois cam to thin ere.

But after all, be it said with complete reverence, the young girl of Nazareth was in much the same state of mind. And it is to her that the fourteenth century boy is speaking.

His descriptions of himself are blunt and boyish and abject and, apart from their occasion, almost contemporaneous, as "have I ben a beste," "I were wurthi my dampnacioun," "I, caityf," "Of verrey right my werk wol me confounde." His very extremities have an all but humorous poignance in them: "Loo, how that theeves sevene chasen mee!" or "Help that my Fader be not wroth with me" or this humanest of all:

And I to him am fals and eek unkynde,
And yit he wole not my dampnacioun—
This thanke I yow, socour of al mankynde!

But if, in the condemnation of himself he is both a realist and a "plain, blunt man," in his Lady's praise he speaks pure poetry, the authentic language of love:

Fleeinge, I flee for socour to thi tente
Me for to hide

with confidence that "Whoso thee loveth, he shal not love in veyn." A very litany one could make of epithets with which he takes his singing way to tell of God's wonders in Mary and the world's deep need of her. "Kalenderes enlumyned ben thei," he says to her in delicate employment of figure, "that in this world ben lighted with thi name." Through Old Testament symbol and New Testament miracle and subsequent devotion, from the burning bush to the Ave Maria he ranges with a freedom and a deference that are wholly youthful and disarming, with a competence and art that are rather more than a metrical exploitation of doctrine. To the devout the *A B C* sounds like prayer, to the critical it sounds like poetry. It is both.

No one pretends that it is great poetry. On the other hand, most readers do not realize how extraordinarily good it really is. For in it a young and comparatively inexperienced Chaucer is confronted with three problems most susceptible alike to pure dullness and poetic paralysis: the task of translation, the inherent formality of prayer, and conventional formality of its vocabulary of title and belief. The first he solves by expanding the line and expanding the spirit of his original. The second he overrides by a surpassing conversational freedom of speech. The third he transfigures by breathing into it at least a poet's breath of faith and love. He takes words that had the life used out of them, as Francis Thompson said of Coleridge, and sets them on their feet, and somehow, at his word they pray and sing. No one doubts that he loved the Lady for whom he did this thing. His songs to her were the admiration of his poet friends. His devotion to her still characterizes him peculiarly. The Hoccleve portrait by which the world best knows him shows him a thoughtful, quiet man with snowy hair and beard and, like his

Prioress, about his arm a pair of beads he bears. Critics say it is his rosary.

This practice of prayer was something of a habit with Chaucer. It is almost the first and last of his work to survive. It was, of course, one of the writers' conventions of his day. Had it not been, there is a probability that he would have practiced it. But, as a convention, the devotional sincerity of his prayers is frequently questioned. Conventions are a badly libelled lot. One knows they are devices; one concludes that they are deceits with an immediacy to be recommended rather for speed than for logic. Particularly is this true of the conventional mediaeval writing. Without going into digression on this matter, it may be volunteered that the fourteenth century writer probably used the convention to say what he meant rather than to say the exact opposite of what he meant. That the form he used is, to us, artificial results not so much from his insincerity as from our own mode of expression. That, to him, would indicate something like savagery. More than once in England the literary convention has achieved militant sincerity and a classic. *Pilgrim's Progress* is a particularly good example for three reasons: It is so completely a convention, so essentially a book of devotion, so sincerely a prayer. It was probably based on the French original of Chaucer's *A B C*. The chances

are that Chaucer meant what he said in his prayers
as in most else that he wrote. If that implies piety,
it is hard to see why, as a quality, that should have
to be explained away. At any rate and in addition
to his early work, as he got into the world of
Christian peoples and practices, he exercised himself upon a number of most moving Christian
prayers. That is, obviously, when he went on
poetic pilgrimage.

The prayers in the *Canterbury Tales* are different in their occasion and import from the
A B C. But like it they are interesting as prayers in
themselves, as sincere and becoming expressions
of an experienced devotion, and more than it, the
poet's profounder power to speak to God of
human needs. For convenience's sake one may con-
sider first his ejaculations, then his citation of
saints, and last, his longer prayers.

The sign of the cross is, of all prayers, the most
appropriate one with which to begin. In the *Man
of Law's Tale*, after the poet's apostrophe to Custance, "the emperoures yonge doghter deere" one
reads that "she blesseth hire"; putting herself
under the protection of that saving sign which was
her hope. In the *Clerk's Tale*, Grisilde gives up
her child without protest, but for comfort "kiste
her sone, and after gan it blesse." Other aspirations
also one meets frequently in the text, used with

congruous reverence: "God so my soule save," "God woot," "for hye Goddes sake," "as God forbade," "God thank it you," "So God you blesse." So kind a convention in so civil an idiom sounds not unpleasant even to impatient modern ears. The name of Christ is used less frequently; "now Jhesu Crist be with you all," and "in name of Crist" appearing only occasionally. This may be due to a reverence of devotion to the Holy Name which tended to express itself in a conservative rather than free use of it. "For Cristes mooder deere," "Crist and his blisful mooder" are only two ejaculations to indicate the central object of mediaeval devotion to whom most of the longer prayers are addressed. "By God and by Saint John" brings one to Chaucer's litany of saints.

Collected and classified, the members of his Church Triumphant include St. Anne, the mother of the Blessed Virgin, the two archangels, Gabriel and Raphael, the precursor John the Baptist, the apostles of eminence, Peter, Paul, James, John the evangelist, Matthew, Mark, and Luke, the great penitents of the early Church, Anthony, Mary of Egypt and Mary Magdalen, with her brother Lazarus, the Roman saints of the household of Cecilia, Pope Urban and the early English saints Frideswide, Cuthbert, Dunstan, Edward, and the boy Hugh of Lincoln. A half dozen others appear possibly for purposes of rime: St. Maurice, St. Giles, St. Clare, St. Martin, St. Ives, St. Joce, St. Ronyon, and "Seint Denyse of Fraunce." St. Valentine appears in his traditional and rather secular role; St. Christopher then as now was being worn on medals; St. Loy enjoyed a pious vogue; St. Julian fostered hospitality; St. Leonard protected captives. St. Kenelm he allows to tell his own dream story in the *Nonnes Priestes Tale*. Scattered through the text, these are a little lost in the human crowd. Gathered as here they are in a group they illustrate the paragraph with their shining. That shining has the warmth of personalities and events splendidly human behind it. Heroism in caring for the sick has earned for St. Julian the name of "hospitalarian" which hearsay hagiography had come to associate rather with social hospitality. His synonymous appearance with the franklin in the *Prologue* can carry with it the compliment of more asceticism than that son of Epicurus can comfortably bear; more, indeed, than Chaucer probably had in mind. He may not have known, either, that the brother of his Breton king, St. Joce, was with his elegant St. Loy on embassy to Dagobert when he protested to tears against even an oath of fidelity. Details so intrinsically unimportant as these contribute constantly to growing richness of our Chaucerian inheritance.

For very proper reasons the poet has included among his saints the two great companion bishops of St. Thomas of Canterbury: St. Augustine and Thomas Bradwardine; and with them the great apologists of east and west: Saints Basil, Chrysostom, Jerome, Augustine, Gregory, and their fellows in spirit and truth: Anselm, Ambrose, Arnold of Villanova, Bernard of Clairvaux, Peter Alphonsus. They are a fair company, judged by the most mundane standards of achievement and eminence. They are a glorified group in that chosen people, the Communion of Saints.

Altogether, these pious aspirations, these pious people bring into the life of the text a brave, bright beauty. They color it, but they do not discolor it. They speak with a sincerity that is not to be mistaken for insincerity. They indicate a faith that can vitalize a figure. Their meaning to the quality of Chaucer's writing can best be found by eliminating them and reading the result. Their meaning to Chaucer cannot be found in quite that way.

The longer prayers involve conditions of anxiety, heartbreak and contrition. They grow out of the life of the context with the inevitability that genius explains, but they grow out of rhetorical conventions only as inevitably beautiful flowers grow out of formal gardens. They are the prayers of a wife, two mothers, and the poet. The prologues of the prioress and her companions will be considered in a chapter of their own. The wife is Dorigen in the *Franklin's Tale,* in that brave endemic battle against the sea that is the tradition and the tragedy of Breton women. Her husband, Arveragus, has been gone from her two years. The sea and the perilous shore that separate them are at once her hope and her distress:

> Is ther no ship, of so manye as I se
> Wol bryngen hom my lord?

she asks herself "ful ofte" alone on that crag-bound coast, from which she turns, in fear and hope, to the promise of the ocean's far horizon. She becomes almost a classic for those who, until the world's end, await their absent ones' return. Her prayer is not less a classic of human reasoning with divine. Thereby it takes aspects of a divine comedy in miniature. Eternal God, she says in effect, you have in your wisdom made nothing useless, but, Lord, these rocks, grizzly and fiendish and black, seem rather a foul confusion of work than the fair creation of such a perfect, wise, and stable God, and then point-blank: "whi han ye wroght this werk unresonable . . . Se ye nat, Lord, how mankynde it destroyeth?" A hundred thousand men have rocks slain, men that are so fair a part of creation, she explains to the deity, made to his "owene merk." How can God's love for men be reconciled with such destruction? Here she can no longer rationalize; "argumentz" she scatters to the "clerkes," announcing "this is my conclusion." She wants her lord safe home.

> . . . wolde God that alle thise rokkes blake
> Were sonken into helle for his sake!
> Thise rokkes sleen myne herte for the feere.

The stunning and ironic answer to her prayer is beside the point. Its candid, conversational attitude toward God, its "hooly Chirches feith" asking the removal of coast range mountains, its genuinely human, and therefore slightly erratic emotion are finely Chaucerian. They illustrate his maturer attitude toward prayer. To appreciate how robust an attitude this is one should read beside it Tennyson's lovely, languorous *Sweet and Low*.

The mothers are Grisilde, the peasant wife of the worthy though capricious Walter, and the noble Roman Dame Custance. The poignancy of their need of prayer leaps to the reader's mind. Brevity may be expected in Grisilde's prayer; it was of the close-knit fabric of her mind. It is a quite tremendous summary of faith and farewell and the heartbreaking payment of her child's life for her own lowliness.

Fareweel my child! I shal thee nevere see.
But sith I thee have marked with the croys
Of thilke Fader—blessed moote he be!—
That for us deyde upon a croys of tree,
Thy soule, litel child, I hym bitake,
For this nyght shaltow dyen for my sake.

A convention that can use the digression of prayer for the mereness of such tragic simplicities and realizations is to be commended for something more than its success as a device.

Dame Custance, in a like position of protagonist, has more to say with the same intensity and faith. Set adrift in a crazy craft off the Surrey coast to die, "she blesseth hire" and invokes the cross of Christ, "O cleere, o welful auter, hooly croys." Addressing "the white Lamb, that hurt was with a spere" she makes, under the circumstances, this least panicky of prayers, "me kepe, and yif me myght my lyf t'amenden." Falsely accused and villainously implicated in murder, she makes her own defense with the splendid eloquence of her proud breeding:

Immortal God, that savedest Susanne
Fro false blame, and thou, merciful mayde,
Marie I meene, doghter to Seint Anne,
Bifore whos child angeles synge Osanne,
If I be giltlees of this felonye,
My socour be, for ellis shal I dye.

However much the stanza may be formed upon the prevailing patterns of rhetoric, it is informed with intensities of innocence and faith. At least, it conveys such intensities to the reader.

A second time banished from the country with her little son in the same derelict boat that brought her there, she prays at her setting out:

> He that me kepte fro the false blame
>
> . . . .
>
> He kan me kepe from harm and eek fro shame
> In salte see, althogh I se noght how.
> In hym triste I, and in his mooder deere.

Comforting her child with "Pees, litel sone," she addresses her prayer to "Mooder . . . mayde bright, Marie." She realizes that in the sum of possible suffering for one's child, her place beside the Mother of Christ is one of contrast:

> Thanne is ther no comparison bitwene
> Thy wo and any wo man may sustene.
> Thow sawe thy child yslayn bifore thyne yen,
> And yet now lyveth my litel child, parfay!

Beyond their depths of motherhood and faith, these simple, human prayers illustrate nothing so much as the sentimental deterioration that marks the printed prayer since Chaucer's day.

These, with the short prayer of the messenger who brings Dame Custance her sentence of banishment, illustrate the longer prayer passages in Chaucer. All are simple, natural, speaking the language of affection but not of affectation, more true to a living Faith than they are to a dead form.

Twice, besides, one finds Chaucer on his knees, so to say: in his passionate plea at the end of *Troilus and Criseyde* to the youth of the world for the changeless love of Christ who "best to love is" and last of all, at the end of his retraction, his thanksgiving to God and his Lady for the simple sum of his good work, a prayer of petition for all the graces of a happy death and heaven at its end from his King Christ, and through the blood of His Sacred Heart.

The first and the last thing that Chaucer wrote was prayer. It finds its proper place in works between. These are fairly convincing evidences of a persistent warp of sincere piety and devotion through all the gay woofs of life and convention that pattern his work. They speak a poet's language. It is a pleasant tongue. It has become almost a lost language.

Chaucer's Nuns

General Prologue

Ther was also a Nonne, a prioresse,
That of hir smylyng was ful symple and coy;
Hire gretteste ooth was but by Seinte Loy;
And she was cleped madame Eglentyne.
Ful weel she soong the service dyvyne,
Entuned in hir nose ful semely,
And Frenssh she spak ful faire and fetisly,
After the scole of Stratford atte Bowe,
For Frenssh of Parys was to hire unknowe.
At mete wel ytaught was she with alle:
She leet no morsel from hir lippes falle,
Ne wette hir fyngres in hir sauce depe;
Wel koude she carie a morsel and wel kepe
That no drope ne fille upon hire brest.
In curteisie was set ful muchel hir lest.
Hir over-lippe wyped she so clene
That in hir coppe ther was no ferthyng sene
Of grece, whan she dronken hadde hir draughte.
Ful semely after hir mete she raughte.
And sikerly she was of greet desport,
And ful plesaunt, and amyable of port,
And peyned hire to countrefete cheere
Of court, and to been estatlich of manere,
And to ben holden digne of reverence.
But, for to speken of hire conscience,

She was so charitable and so pitous
She wolde wepe, if that she saugh a mous
Kaught in a trappe, if it were deed or bledde.
Of smale houndes hadde she that she fedde
With rosted flessh, or milk and wastel-breed.
But soore wepte she if oon of hem were deed,
Or if men smoot it with a yerde smerte;
And al was conscience and tendre herte.
Ful semyly hir wympul pynched was;
Hir nose tretys, hir eyen greye as glas,
Hir mouth ful smal, and therto softe and reed;
But sikerly she hadde a fair forheed;
It was almoost a spanne brood, I trowe;
For, hardily, she was nat undergrowe.
Ful fetys was hir cloke, as I was war.
Of smal coral aboute hire arm she bar
A peire of bedes, gauded al with grene,
And theron heng a brooch of gold ful sheene,
On which ther was first write a crowned A,
And after *Amor vincit omnia.*

Another NONNE with hire hadde she,
That was hir chapeleyne, and preestes thre.
                    (*The Canterbury Tales* 1 (A) 118-164)

Chaucer's Nuns

THE NUNS in the *Canterbury Tales* are characters around whom a proverbially romantic interest and an unproverbial set of difficulties gather. They are, like their twenty-seven companions on the pilgrimage, typical individuals of their class, seen through the fixating medium of Chaucer's personality; seen by us through the less luminous distance of five hundred years. Criticism seems to have followed methods of microscopic analysis of them out of their habitual environment rather than telescopic synthesis of them in their environment. The problems they present are acutely psychological and prosaically human. Let us come to the matter in this wise.

Before one can attempt an understanding either of Chaucer's Nuns or, indeed, of himself as artist in creating them, one must know in part the material on which he worked. A Nun, Religious, Sister—whichever name you wish—is not merely a woman in a "cloke ful fetys" and "ful semely pynched . . . wimple," nor even a woman upon whom the religious life has been superimposed, but a woman whose life has undergone a change more subtle and entirely spiritual than marriage but quite as real. The absolute proof of this statement is experience; the strongest ulterior proof is the word of one who has had this experience, corroborated by the whole world's recognition of the religious state. The forces by which this change is effected are two: the first, a mystical but most real relation between the soul and God; the second, the rules and customs and religious practices of the particular community in which the individual seeks to perfect that mystical relation. These determine almost entirely, apart from the personality of the individual, the manners, the deportment, the whole external aspect of the religious. So apparent are the effects that religious communities recognize among themselves their outstanding qualities and characterize one another by them. The point I wish to make clear is this: Chaucer in depicting the Nuns was not dealing merely with women wearing a particular and conspicuous costume, symbolic of religion, but women whose whole selves had undergone a subtle change by reason of the two influences just named. He was representing the visible effects of a spiritual life of which he had no experimental or vicarious knowledge. That fact should be italicized in considering critically his accomplished task. And— which is almost more important—the Nuns themselves, to be interpreted at all, must be interpreted in relation to their Rule, their customs, and the community prayers by which their entire lives were regulated. Such an interpretation of Chaucer's Nuns this chapter proposes to make.

The Prioress and her chaplain were, according to Chaucer's allusion, members of the convent at Stratford at Bow, a Benedictine abbey of note and prominence in the fourteenth century. This means that they were living under the *Rule of St. Benedict,* that their exterior conduct was regulated by the norm and pattern laid down in it, and that their interior or spiritual life reflected its spirit as it fed and thrived upon the religious practices prescribed in it. Chief among these practices was the chanting of the Divine Office to which we shall come presently. What their exterior was we learn from the *Prologue*; what their interior life must have been we can guess from the spirituality of their own prologues and stories proper, unconscious as their breathing and quite as natural. Now for an interpretation of these through the *Rule of St. Benedict*.

Logically we begin with the Prioress as she appears in the *Prologue*, and we look to her holy rule rather than to any other source book for direction upon her smiling, her oath, her name, her singing, her table manners—well nigh threadbare with much quoting—her charity, her pets, her cloak and beads and brooch, her age—mind you—and her chaplain; everything in fact except her face, which is after Chaucer's best conventional pattern.

To interpret her "smyling . . . ful symple and coy" I would go sooner to the *Rule of St. Benedict*, with which Chaucer was easily familiar, than to the pastorelle of the fourteenth century where Professor Lowes hunts the phrase with such characteristic thoroughness.[1]

For in the Northern Verse version one reads:

> A priores hir fast sal breke,
> And silence, when scho suld not speke,
> To myrth hir gestes in that scho may.[2]

The prose translated by D. Oswald Hunter Blair corresponds: "When, therefore, a guest is announced, let him be met by the Superior or the brethren, with all due charity . . . When the guests have been received . . . let the Superior, or anyone he may appoint, sit with them . . . The Superior may break his fast for the sake of the guest . . . Let the Abbot pour water on the hands of the guests; and himself as well as the whole community, wash their feet." Chapter LIII.

Considering that this is the spirit of the rule

---

[1] J. L. Lowes, "Simple and Coy," *Anglia*, XXXIII, 440-451.
[2] *Three Middle English Versions of the Rule of St. Benedict*, Chap. LI, 103.

under which the Prioress had enlisted, one feels that her smiling was the minimum of hospitality which she must have felt for strangers, at home or abroad, and one understands her congeniality and cheer later remarked as a part of the same spirit.

Her lovely and romantic name is a sure target for remark. It is exactly what a little girl would be like to call her favorite doll. How did Chaucer hit upon it? By much the same process, I should think, as leads any author to prefer Anita to Hannah, or Eloise to Ella, as the name of his heroine. There is no written rule, so far as I know, for the giving of names in religious communities. It is a matter determined by custom, which is a form of written or unwritten practice in all communities, almost as binding as the rule and harder to depart from. In regard to names, three customs prevail. In some communities, the Sisters retain their family names, and Mary or Elizabeth or Susan Eglantine becomes in religion Madame Eglantine. This is not, I think, the practice of the Benedictines. Other communities, usually small ones, allow the prospective Sister to choose her own name. In most large communities the subject has no actual choice; she or her friends may express a wish in the matter, which may or may not be considered. However, the name given is either the whole or a part of a saint's name or bears traditions of sanctity. Magdalen is a familiar example, taken not from Mary, the sister of Martha and Lazarus, but from Magdala, her home. What clouds of sanctity trail from Madame Eglantine's name are lost in the mists of a hagiography more familiar to Chaucer than to me. At all events its chances of being "self-chosen" are two to one, and if self-chosen, the chooser was Chaucer. That his choice was a canny one, I admit, with the canniness of a journalist.

I have thought it unnecessary to speak of Madame Eglantine's negative oath, in view of Professor Hales' and Professor Lowes' articles on it.[3] The singing of the divine service contains two interesting bits of unexhausted inference. A word first in regard to the Office itself may be illuminating. Aside from the Mass, the Divine Office, or "service" as Chaucer calls it, is the most solemn liturgical prayer of the Church. It is composed chiefly of the psalms, arranged in seven parts with prose prayers and hymns appropriately introduced. The seven parts are: Matins and Lauds which are said late in the afternoon (by anticipation) or in cloistered orders, shortly after

[3] J. W. Hales, "Chaucer's Prioress's 'Greatest Oath,'" *The Athenaeum*, Jan. 10, 1891, 54. J. L. Lowes, "The Prioress's Oath," *Romanic Review*, v. No. 4.

midnight; Prime, Tierce, Sexte, and None recited during the morning hours, and Vespers in the afternoon or evening, followed by a postlude, so to say, called Compline. The Office is in Latin and is chanted and intoned, "entuned in the nose," in various keys. It is recited daily by all priests and chanted in choir in such monastic orders as the Benedictines, the Carthusians, the Carmelites. A shorter form of the same solemn prayer of the Church, known as the *Little Office, Little Hours of the Blessed Virgin,* or *Psalter,* was used during the Middle Age by the laity and is still used by all religious orders that do not recite the Divine Office. The Office is chanted by the community together or "in choir," ordinarily, but when religious are on journeys they recite their office "privately"; that is, they read it to themselves. *The Rule of St. Benedict,* Chapter XIX, says on this subject: "Loke ye do yure seruise als ye stode by-fore god almihti. And lokis, when ye sing, that yure herte acorde wid yure voice; than sing ye riht." And, in truth, it is a matter of conscience with every religious to intone the Office "ful semely," as it is the most important of all vocal prayers.

Here are the bare facts; now for their two promised inferences. First, Chaucer must have been familiar with the Divine Office, so familiar that he knew how it should be said. That he knew even better the Little Office will appear in the discussion of the *Prioress's Prologue* later. Second, he must have been at some convent for only there could he have heard the "service divyne entuned." His statement regarding the Prioress in this connection evidently refers to her life in the cloister; no religious recites the Office aloud when traveling. One might go further and infer that through business or ties of kinship[4] he must have been well acquainted with some community; a stranger or a casual visitor does not ordinarily hear the religious chanting the Office, or if he does, he is not able to interpret it as Chaucer does. This inference reinforces a theory offered later as to the possible unwritten source of the Nuns' stories.

One comes rather resentfully to the table manners of the Prioress upon which so much trivial comment has been expended. I will connect her "cloke . . . ful fetis" with her conduct at table, as having no slight bearing upon it. The *Rule*, Chapter LVI, makes this provision for clothing:

> In comun places for alkins note
> Sufficis a kirtil and a cote;
> And mantels sal thai haue certayn,
> In winter dubil, in somer playne . . .

[4] Lounsbury, *Studies in Chaucer*, I, 100.

And when thai sal went in cuntre,
    [i.e., on a journey]
Thair clething sal mor honest be; . . .

And home agayn when thai cum eft,
Then sal thai were slik os thai left.

Here is explicit provision for the "fetis" cloak,
and a homely, human reason for the Prioress's
carefulness at table. She was wearing not only a
clean, but a new habit, which she would be expected to give up on her return to her convent.
Is it any wonder that she was so effectively solicitous "that no drope ne fille up-on hir brest"? I
can well understand how Chaucer might have mis-
interpreted such apparent over-daintiness, and
how critics have found it affected, even "a little
ridiculous."[5] But none of them ever wore a religious habit, nor had the least idea of what real
distress a Sister feels at getting a spot on her habit,
especially at table. Her habit is holy to her: "a spot
without is a spot within" is among the most vener-
able of community proverbs, and St. Bernard's
"I love poverty always but dirt never" is applied
to clothing almost more than to anything else in
religious life. This highly cultivated antipathy
for dirt accounts more reasonably for the dainty

[5] R. K. Root, *The Poetry of Chaucer*, 190.

details of Madame Eglantine's conduct at table than affectation or an aping of the manners of the world, the "chere of court," two things that are anathema in the spirit of every religious community.

One other determining element in the Prioress's character that even Chaucer might not have been able to account exactly for but which would manifest itself surely at table was her spirit of mortification. The veriest novice knows that mortification is the mainspring of religious life and bodily mortification is practiced in some measure by all religious at table. St. Benedict says: "Let two dishes, then, suffice for all the brethren . . . For there is nothing so adverse to a Christian as gluttony, according to the words of our Lord: 'See that your hearts be not overcharged with surfeiting.' " Chapter XXXIX. This may suggest a new meaning to the line, "ful semely after hir mete she raughte."

The "rosted flesh, and milk and wastel-breed" for the "smale houndes" is an open extravagance except that these were gathered from the table after the meal was over. And this custom is as old as St. Francis and his brother Wolf, I suspect. Personally, I see every day of my life a Sister with as "tendre a herte" as the Prioress—an old Sister, by the way—gathering choice bits of meat and creamy milk for our excellent mouser, Fluff, and

scattering "wastel breed" to the little warblers and
finches around our door. I should say that this
good Sister's heart goes out to the canine world
to such degree that more than one "hounde"
greets her with barks of joy. One would have to
live in a convent to appreciate fully what Chaucer
has really done in these sixty lines of the *Prologue.*

The well-pinched wimple is one of the most
interesting details of the Prioress's dress. No one
who has ever seen a Benedictine habit can miss its
significance. The wimple or collar of this habit
is as typical as the coronet of the Sister of Charity,
if not quite as architectural. It is of white linen,
accordion plaited or "pinched" to fit closely
around the neck and over the shoulders in such
manner that each plait forms a circle and the
whole wimple is a series of concentric circles. The
mystery of its achievement might well defy the
feminine mind; its neat and supple tidiness would
scarce escape even the masculine eye. Small
wonder, then, that Chaucer directs the attention
of five hundred years to the well-pinched wimple.
It was a feature of the Nun's habit to elicit admiration from the least observant. Suggestions of vanity
on the Nun's part arise, it seems to me, from a lack
of understanding of a Sister's attitude toward her
habit. It is a matter not of vanity but of duty to

her to wear it modestly and becomingly as the uniform of her high vocation. Here, again, a secular point of view fails to catch the chief significance of things that may have deceived even Chaucer.

On the subject of the "smal coral . . . peire of bedes" one might expand into a brief history of the origin and use of prayer beads. Let it suffice here to say that since the thirteenth century such beads have been in common use among religious and lay persons alike. At that time they were called Paternosters, from the prayer most often said on them. Their manufacturers, Paternosterers, were a recognized craft guild. Stephen Boyleau in his *Livres des Métiers* gives full details of the four guilds of "Patenotriers" in Paris in 1268. Paternoster Row in London commemorates the gathering place of a group of these same craftsmen. The prayer beads that the Prioress carried were the work of medieval handicraft rather than twentieth-century machines, an explanation quite sufficient to account for their exquisite beauty. Only one who has seen the large variety of beads in common use among Catholics can appreciate how lovely this particular pair must have been. The spirit of poverty would forbid a Sister to-day to use anything so elaborate, but in the days when things were not merely useful but beautiful, this pair of beads may not have been such an extravagance.

The suggestion that even Chaucer had in mind an ambiguous meaning for the motto, "Amor vincit omnia," or an eye to its cheaper journalistic value seems to me unworthy and inconsistent with his attitude of pronounced respect toward the Prioress. As a matter of fact, this is one of the commonest of epigrams among religious, and I know that one could find it worked in cross stitch, or painted in all the varying forms of realistic and conventional art and framed as a motto in dozens of our convents in our very unmystical and unmedieval United States to-day. I have no doubt that Chaucer himself had seen it so in some convent parlor, possibly in Norfolk where a ring bearing the same inscription has been unearthed and where there was a large Benedictine convent in Chaucer's time.[6] It is, in three words, the most typical motto that could have been engraved upon the brooch.

The "brooch" itself, hanging from the beads, was undoubtedly a medal, one of the commonest sacramentals in the Catholic Church. It is a small object, much like a locket, bearing engraving and inscriptions of a religious nature. In itself it has no virtue; its value lies in the fact that it reminds

[6] *Life Records of Chaucer*, 111 (2d series), 135.

the owner or bearer of some truth of religion and so inspires him to virtue. Medals are of unlimited variety and number and purpose. They are made of gold, silver, plated or oxidized metals, cloisonné, bronze, or cheaper substances and range from simple crudeness to exquisite beauty in workmanship and design. The Prioress's "broche" is a good, but not an over-elaborate, medal.

So much for the accidents of Madame Eglantine's exterior. The discussion of them has been neither scholarly nor pretentious; it has regarded them simply in the light of the Prioress's Rule, under a modified form of which the writer herself lives, and in that light has indicated details that the most luminous of old manuscripts might not shed upon them.

One other matter remains before leaving the *Prologue*: the question of the gentle Madame's age. By what evidence or inference critics conclude that the Prioress was young I do not know. Professor Lowes, referring to the touches of artistry in the details of description, remarks on "the skill with which they suggest still youthful flesh and blood behind the well pinched wimple. Not only in his account of the amiable foibles of the Prioress," he continues, "but in his choice of words and phrases, Chaucer suggests the delightfully imperfect submergence of the woman in the nun." Which implies, if it does not state, that she was, more than probably, young. The emphasis I understand, is upon the nice perfection of Chaucer's workmanship and art. But from that very point of view I believe that there is a failure to appreciate his greater perfection. He has given us someone much harder to paint with his brush of words than a young Nun in whom the young woman is as yet imperfectly submerged. That task might have tempted his immaturity. But here is his picture of a woman a decade or more beyond middle age (my opinion) sweetened and spiritually transformed by the rules and religious practices of her choice, who can be in the world without being of it, gracious without affectation, and friendly without boldness. That she combines the wisdom of the serpent with the simplicity of the dove one realizes from her exquisite rebuke to the shipman when, in telling her story, she has occasion to refer to an abbot, and remembering his "daun John" she puts in her artless aside, "a holy man, as monkes been, or elles oughten be."[7] Personally, I think that a younger Nun would have expressed open resentment or have kept silence on the subject; only a mature woman of experience and courage and tact could have made

[7] K. Bregy, "The Inclusiveness of Chaucer," *Catholic World*, June, 1922.

and used an opportunity for a well-earned repri-
mand with such casual sweetness. She is a woman,
evidently, who has taken to heart the Pauline
lesson of becoming all things to all men, and
learned it well. It is one of the ideals of all religious
life, and it seems more natural to think that her
"greet disport" and "amiable port" are the out-
come of it rather than "compounded" like "her
character," as Professor Root says, "of many affec-
tations."[8] The cheerful, dignified, kindly woman
of fifty years, perhaps, is what the religious reads
out of Chaucer's Prioress, and she is decidedly a
more complex character to penetrate and portray
than a Sister with the natural gayety and exuber-
ance of youth still about her.

One turns to the *Rule of St. Benedict* for some
stipulation as to the age requirement for the office
of Prioress. In the Northern Prose Version, Chapter LI, one reads, "The yung sall onur thalde,
and the alde salle lufe the yunge. Nane sal calle
othir by thaire name, but the priures sal calle
thaim hir 'sistirs.' The abbesse, for sho es in godis
stede, sal be callid 'dame.' " This might imply,
from its context, seniority; but in the Caxton ab-
stract one finds: "Such (Superiors) owe not to be
chosen therto by their age, but for their wertuous
lyuing and wysdom, chastyte and sobre dealying,

[8] R. K. Root, *The Poetry of Chaucer*, 190.

and also for their pyte and mercy, the whyche they
must vse in all their dedys." Then follows a list
of other qualities that are the very reverse of
youthful virtues; prudence, for example, com-
passion, patience, industry, great and all-embrac-
ing charity. We are not to suppose that the Prioress
or any other Superior ever embodies them all,
but one looks for and finds more of these requisites
in an old than in a young person.

Other proofs of the Prioress's age are not difficult to find, proofs almost absurd in their home-
liness. Most religious rules or customs even to-day
forbid the keeping of pet animals. One remembers
the terse injunction in the *Ancren Riwle,* "Ye
shall not possess any beast, my dear Sisters, except
only a cat." That abuses to this regulation grew
up Grosseteste's comments leave no small doubt;
a fact of more significance to us, however, is that
when an exception to the rule is made, it is ordinarily in favor of an older religious. A Sister of
fifty or sixty can have a bird or a dog or a cat with
propriety; a Sister of thirty would scarcely think
of such a thing. So do the "smale houndes" betray
the age of their gentle mistress.

This point may be too trivial to be of value;
if it will serve no other purpose we may "use it for
our mirth, yea, for our laughter." Chaucer says the
Prioress

>   was so charitable and so pitous
> She wolde wepe, if that she saw a mous
> Kaught in a trappe.

Human nature in respect to mice has not changed since those days. No young Nuns that I have ever met, and they are many, would have been moved to tears at such a sight; most of them would certainly have screamed or have wanted to.

So the age of the Prioress rests, like Chaucer's own, an unknown quantity of continued speculation. For the unchivalry of exposing these evidences of her advanced age, we offer the high security of the maiden on the Grecian urn, "she cannot fade."

The presence of the Prioress's companion is in strict accord with apostolic tradition and is followed closely in most religious communities. One is startled to hear her spoken of as a chaplain, a name ordinarily applied to priests. An article published by Dr. Furnivall in the *Academy* some years ago clears up the difficulty by explaining that the nun-chaplain is a regular office in Benedictine convents.[9] And so the last difficulty in the *Prologue* disappears.

One quotation more from the Benedictine Rule will be of service in completing what I have

[9] F. J. Furnivall, "Chaucer's Prioress's Nun-Chaplain," *Academy*, May 22, 1880, 385. Also in *Anglia*, IV, 238.

pompously called a telescopic synthesis of Chaucer's Nuns in their environment. It is the rule on journeys. "Let the brethren who are about to be sent on a journey commend themselves to the prayers of all the brethren and of the Abbot, and at the last prayer of the Work of God let a commemoration always be made of the absent. (A custom still practiced in communities.) Let the brethren that return from a journey, on the very day that they come back, lie prostrate on the floor of the Oratory at all the Canonical Hours . . . and beg the prayers of all on account of their transgressions, in case they should perchance upon the way have seen or heard anything harmful, or fallen into idle talk. And let no one presume to relate to another what he may have seen or heard outside the Monastery; for thence arise manifold evils." Chapter LXVII. This completes the portion of the Rule by which the Nuns in Chaucer and their conduct on the way to Canterbury should be judged. It is quoted to give some idea of the spirit in which a Prioress and her companion would undertake such a journey and what would be their responsibilities in regard to it. Nothing but a very urgent spiritual quest could have induced them to leave their cloister and join so worldly and public an excursion. It may be urged that the Rule was subject to many abuses, as no doubt it was, but nowhere does Chaucer give us any reason to think that his Nuns were of a tramp or derelict order; the reverence and courtesy of which he specifically says they were worthy is proof enough that he was depicting the typical "ninety-nine who need not penance" Sister rather than the well advertised one who does.

At the beginning of this study it was suggested that a fruitful and nearer-to-truth study of Chaucer's Nuns could be made by viewing them in the light of their rules, customs, and community prayers than by the measure of a social life that they had voluntarily abandoned. The Nuns as they appear in the *Prologue* are chiefly viewed from the outside; one sees them here as they have been molded and fashioned by their rule. That rule has been applied to every detail of their description and in most cases has yielded a more human, if not a different, understanding of them. Putting these parts together and viewing the united whole through the kindly telescope of our common human nature we get in the Nuns of Chaucer's *Prologue* more lovable characters and immeasurably finer creations than critical analysis shows us.

II

Thus far we have considered the Nuns as a psychological and spiritual product of the rules and customs of St. Benedict; in the *Prologues* to their *Tales* and their stories proper we will regard them under the influence of their daily prayers. As has already been explained, all the older religious orders recite the Divine Office every day and have done so since the beginning of monasticism. They live in the spirit of this solemn, liturgical prayer with which their day's labor is punctuated and their night's rest broken. Beside the Holy Mass, it is the great thing for which they live. This may seem an extravagant saying to the secular world, but one need only go to a cloistered convent to find it verified. The lives of the religious become colored by it; their very speech takes on the phraseology of the psalms and hymns that make up their daily converse with the Most High.

To point the truth of this, one turns to the two Prologues, spoken by the Nuns. The Prioress begins, "O Lord, our Lord" which critics have had no difficulty in identifying with the opening verse of the Eighth Psalm. Scholars have also recognized the *Salve Regina,* the *Memento Rerum Conditor,* and other hymns of the Church in passages of the two Prologues. But they have not seen that the two Nuns are merely paraphrasing in them the parts of the morning Office in which the Blessed Virgin is invoked; or, in other words speaking the language of praise most natural to them. Just here is an interesting detail. Chaucer makes his excerpts, not from the Divine, but from the Little Office. The reason is easy. He was more familiar with it and knew that all the psalms and prayers it contained were included in the longer Office which the Nuns actually said.

At the risk of being tiresome I will make the parallel. The first seven lines of the *Prioress's Prologue* are a paraphrase of the first three verses of the opening psalm of Matins. Then follows seven lines in which the Prioress combines an antiphon of Matins, "Vouchsafe that I may praise thee, O sacred Virgin; give me strength against my enemies," with her own particular task of story telling and her intention in it. This matter of expressing one's intention in the performance of every act, no matter how trivial or indifferent in nature, is also a fundamental practice of religious life and is based on St. Paul's injunction "Whether you eat or drink or whatever else you do, do all for the honor and glory of God." As one progresses in her task, she renews her intention in order to increase her merit in the performance of it. This explains the renewed ejaculations of both Nuns as they proceed with their stories. This may sound like pure fiction, but again I refer to any and all religious communities in the world for corroboration, or to *The Imitation of Christ* for that mat-

ter. Even pupils in Catholic schools are taught
and exhorted to offer all their actions to God
directly or through the medium of the Blessed
Virgin or the Saints, and such an offering is part
of every well-instructed Catholic's morning prayer.

To return to the Prologue: the third stanza, beginning "O mooder Mayde!" is a free form of the
third long antiphon in Lauds, the part of the
Office following Matins—"In the bush which
Moses saw burning without being consumed, we
acknowledge the preservation of thy admirable
virginity. O holy Mother of God, make interces-
sion for us." The fourth stanza goes back to the
prayer and Absolution of Matins which are: "O
holy and immaculate virginity, I know not with
what praises to extol thee," and, "By the prayers
and merits of the blessed Mary ever Virgin and
of all the Saints, may the Lord bring us to the
kingdom of heaven." The fifth stanza seems to be
the Prioress's renewal of her intention, in her own
words, and is a perfect reflection of numberless
such daily improvised prayers.

The Prologue of the Second Nun's Tale takes us
back to the *Rule of St. Benedict* where one reads
many very positive injunctions against idleness, a
vice scrupulously avoided by the large majority
of religious, all rumors of lazy monks and idle
nuns to the contrary notwithstanding. St. Bene-

dict says: "Idilnesse is the enmye of the soule, wherfore lyke as the couent ben occupyed certeyn howres aboute the seruice of god, soo certeyn other howres ben thei occupyed in redyng and studyeng of heuenly thynges, and in laboures wyth theyr body." Whatever convention Chaucer was following in this mild invective against idleness as a proem to the Nun's story[10] he is, consciously or unconsciously, making her live according to her rule and supplying her with legitimate and ordered occupation against the evil of idleness, "reading . . . of heavenly things."

As to the Invocation, I like to find its sources in the Little Office as much as in Macrobius and Dante, sufficient as they may be to account for it.[11] The opening represents the nun's expression of her intention, without which no religious ever undertakes any work of importance. It follows in spirit and loosely in words, the *Sacrosanctae* and the *Invitatory* of Matins. The hymn *Quem terra, pontus, sidera* which follows immediately in the Office is paraphrased, as Professor Lowes has pointed out in the next twenty lines of the Invocation.

By applying the test of the Little Office to the

[10] Carleton Brown, "Prologue of Chaucer's 'Life of St. Cecile,'" *Modern Philology*, IX, 1-16.

[11] J. L. Lowes, "The Second Nun's Prologue, Alonus and Macrobius," *Modern Philology*, XV, 193.

two Prologues of the Nuns' Tales, we find that they embody in spirit, frequently in word, the opening and closing prayer (*Salve Regina*) of Matins and Lauds; that is, the prayer with which the Nuns' daily life began. The most pertinent and significant point in this study is, I think, the recognition of the part the Office played in the lives of the Prioress and her companion and the natural overflow of its most beautiful and fitting parts into their more worldly speech. Chaucer may not have known just how deep this undercurrent was; in which case the more glory to him for representing what he observed but did not understand was an outward expression of the very essence of religious devotion.

III

The Nuns' stories themselves have been carefully traced by any number of Chaucerian scholars.[12] What suggestions are here volunteered arise from homely experience rather than from scholarly research and may be worth nothing. It is abundantly evident to any reader, to the re-

[12] Carleton Brown, "Chaucer's Prioresses Tale and Its Analogues," *Publications, Modern Language Association*, XXI, 486; "Chaucer's 'Litel Clergeon,'" *Modern Philology*, 111, 467; "Chaucer and the Hours of the Blessed Virgin," *Modern Language Notes*, XXX, 231; J. L. Lowes, "The 'Corones Two' of the Second Nun's Tale," *Publications, Modern Language Association*, XXVI, 315; F. Tupper, "Chaucer and the Prymer," *Modern Language Notes*, XXX, 9.

ligious most of all, that Chaucer knew personally,
even intimately, Sisters; not only that, he had
talked with many of them, I should say; had
listened to their stories, begun and ended and
interspersed with pious ejaculations. Whether he
got the text of the little clergeon from Gautier,
or Caesarius, or the Paris Beggar Boy or the unknown X is a point on which research may ponder
futilely; but that he knew the story from the lips
of some old Nun before he knew any of these
would not surprise me in the least. Such a source
may be the missing manuscript X, of the existence
of which Professor Carleton Brown seems to have
no doubt. It is much easier for me to trace the
"maternal touches of human motherhood" in that
inspired passage.

> My litel child, now wol I fecche thee,
> Whan that the greyn is fro thy tonge y take;
> Be nat agast, I wol thee nat forsake!

referred to in "Some Old French Miracles of
Our Lady"[13] to a real flesh-and-blood Sister, a
Benedictine no doubt, than to the cold and frag-
mentary offerings of age-old ink and paper. For
the potential but foregone motherhood of the
consecrated virgin has always found outlets in such

[13] W. M. Hart, *The C. M. Gayley Anniversary Papers, U. of C.
Publications in Modern Philology,* XI.

expressions of ardent, spiritualized tenderness. Cold print cannot convince one of this fact but a ten minutes' conversation with any Sister who has grown old gracefully in religion will do it without fail. This is, of course, more suggestive than scholarly, but may lead to new clues and methods of approach.

I like to think of Chaucer, the child, a "little clergeon" himself, perhaps, or later "his felaw" listening again and again to the stories of the childish singer of the *Alma Redemptoris,* of the "corones two," and of the martyrdom of St. Cecilia from the lips of some dear old Sister, an aunt or a grandaunt, perhaps—who knows? They are just the stories that Sisters are telling to the smaller and even the grown children in Catholic boarding schools the world over to-day; they are the stories that the children clamor for again and again and never tire of hearing. It was there that I heard them before I knew of Goeffrey Chaucer; and the Nuns' tales took me back, not to manuscripts, nor sermons, nor even to the lives of the saints, but to the stories told by Sisters in our recreations at boarding school. There are seventeen most impressionable years of Chaucer's life unexplored. One need suppose that only once during that time he visited a convent and the rest is easy. No child ever ventured in wide-eyed awe into a convent corridor but some motherly old Nun broke through the barrier of his shyness with a battery of just such stories.

To return to the little clergeon, the lines

> And eek also, where as he saugh th'ymage
> Of Cristes mooder, hadde he in usage,
> As hym was taught, to knele adoun and seye
> His *Ave Marie*, as he goth by the weye.

are like a casual remark upon a custom still common in all convent schools and Catholic churches to-day. A host of "little clergeons" can be seen before statues of Our Lady saying their Ave Maria now as in the days of the small singer of "Asie."

The *Alma Redemptoris* of his devotion I am inclined to believe was that of Hermanus Contractus (Alma Redemptoris quae pervia coeli) because of its greater familiarity among the Catholic laity; more especially because it is sung during Advent, the time precisely when the little lad heard and learned it.

This one other unscholarly suggestion upon the Prioress's Tale may or may not be of value. From my first reading of the story many years ago, I have always taken the *greyn* laid upon the child's tongue to mean the consecrated Host. This, I realize, is a perfectly private interpretation on which no fact can be based. But, investigating, I have found this much to substantiate my strange notion. *Greyn* is defined by *Bradley and Murray* to have meant in early usage "a small part." The Host is often called a "particle" and is given in the dictionary as one meaning for "particle." So, without any twisting of definitions, the *greyn* could mean the Holy Communion. The sequel is interesting. In the life of St. Stanislaus Kostka, a sixteenth century copy of the little clergeon, we read that Our Lady appeared to him several times, accompanied by angels, who in times of persecution twice brought him Holy Communion.[14]

One other meaning for *greyn* in *Bradley and Murray* ought to be considered here. It was a common word for bead, prayer bead. As such beads were most commonly used to count Ave Marias upon, it seems evident that if the *greyn* was not the consecrated particle, it must have been the bead of the angelic salutation.

A suggestion regarding St. Cecilia's angel and another about the crown and then this paper will have an end. Nowhere have I found an explanation of Cecilia's speech, "I have an angel which loveth me," but it is not far to seek. It refers quite evidently to the Catholic teaching of a guardian angel, based upon the first verse of Psalm 91: "He hath given his angels charge over thee"; and the

[14] C. C. Martindale, *Christ's Cadets*, 74, 75, 82, 95.

words of Christ, spoken of little children: "Their angels see the face of my Father Who is in heaven."

The symbolism of the colors, red and white, has been most carefully worked out by Professor Lowes in the article on the two crowns to which I have already referred. These references to the Canticle of Canticles merely emphasize his point: "My beloved is white and ruddy, chosen out of thousands"; V-10; and everywhere in this same mystical song lilies are spoken of as the abiding place of the most chaste and rapturous of all lovers.

IV

This long hunt amid the quiet places of the Benedictine Rule and Office for rare Chaucerian birds is over. How far it has frightened from their coverts shy and unexpected fledglings I cannot guess. If it has served so much as to open up to the scholar new woods and fields in which to range, it will have been a "moste dere" chase.

The Cleansing of Man's Soul

The Parson's Tale

OURE sweete Lord God of hevene, that no man wole perisse, but wole that we comen alle to the knoweleche of hym, and to the blisful lif that is perdurable,/ amonesteth us by the prophete Jeremie, that seith in thys wyse:/ Stondeth upon the weyes, and seeth and axeth of olde pathes (that is to seyn, of olde sentences) which is the goode wey,/ and walketh in that wey, and ye shal fynde refresshynge for youre soules, etc./ Manye been the weyes espirituels that leden folk to oure Lord Jhesu Crist, and to the regne of glorie./ Of whiche weyes, ther is a ful noble wey and a ful covenable, which may nat fayle to man ne to womman that thurgh synne hath mysgoon fro the righte wey of Jerusalem celestial;/ and this wey is cleped Penitence, of which man sholde gladly herknen and enquere with al his herte,/ to wyten what is Penitence, and whennes it is cleped Penitence, and in how manye maneres been the acciouns or werkynges of Penitence,/ and how manye speces ther been of Penitence, and whiche thynges apertenen and bihoven to Penitence, and whiche thynges destourben Penitence./

Seint Ambrose seith that Penitence is the pleynynge of man for the gilt that he hath doon, and namoore to do any thyng for which hym oghte to pleyne./ And som doctour seith, "Penitence is the waymentynge of man that sorweth for his synne, and pyneth hymself for he hath mysdoon."/ Penitence, with certeyne circumstances, is verray repentance of a man that halt hymself in sorwe and oother peyne for his giltes./ And for he shal be verray penitent, he shal first biwaylen the synnes that he hath doon, and stidefastly purposen in his herte to have shrift of mouthe, and to doon satisfacioun,/ and nevere to doon thyng for which hym oghte moore to biwayle or to compleyne, and to continue in goode werkes, or elles his repentance may nat availle./ For, as seith seint Ysidre, "he is a japere and a gabbere, and no verray repentant, that eftsoone dooth thyng for which hym oghte repente."/ Wepynge, and nat for to stynte to do synne, may nat avayle./ But natheless, men shal hope that every tyme that man falleth, be it never so ofte, that he may arise thurgh Penitence, if he have grace; but certeinly it is greet doute./ For, as seith Seint Gregorie, "unnethe ariseth he out of his synne, that is charged with the charge of yvel usage."/ And therfore repentant folk, that stynte for to synne, and forlete synne er that synne forlete hem, hooly chirche holdeth hem siker of hire savacioun./ And he that synneth and verraily repenteth hym in his laste end, hooly chirche yet hopeth his savacioun, by the grete mercy of oure Lord Jhesu Crist, for his repentaunce; but taak the siker wey./

And now, sith I have declared yow what thyng is Penitence, now shul ye understonde that ther been three acciouns of Penitence./ The firste is that a man be baptized after that he hath synned./ Seint Augustyn seith "But he be penytent for his olde synful lyf, he may nat bigynne the newe clene lif."/ For, certes, if he be baptized withouten penitence of his olde gilt, he receyveth the mark of baptesme, but nat the grace ne the remission of his synnes, til he have repentance verray./ Another defaute is this, that men doon deedly synne after that they han receyved baptesme./ The thridde defaute is that men fallen in venial synnes after hir baptesme, fro day to day./ Therof seith Seint Augustyn that penitence of goode and humble folk is the penitence of every day./

The speces of Penitence been three. That oon of hem is solempne, another is commune, and the thridde is privee./ Thilke penance that is solempne is in two maneres; as to be put out of hooly chirche in Lente, for slaughtre of children, and swich maner thyng./ Another is, whan a man hath synned openly, of which synne the fame is openly spoken in the contree, and thanne hooly chirche by juggement destreyneth hym for to do open penaunce./ Commune penaunce is that preestes enjoynen men in certeyn caas, as for to goon peraventure naked in pilgrimages, or bare-foot./ Pryvee penaunce is thilke that men doon alday for privee synnes, of whiche we shryve us prively and receyve privee penaunce./

Now shaltow understande what is bihovely and necessarie to verray perfit Penitence. And this stant on three thynges:/ Contricioun of herte, Confessioun of Mouth, and Satisfaccioun./ For which seith Seint John Crisostom: "Penitence destreyneth a man to accepte benygnely every peyne that hym is enjoyned, with contricioun of herte, and shrift of mouth, with satisfaccioun; and in werkynge of alle manere humylitee."/ And this is fruytful penitence agayn three thynges in whiche we wratthe oure Lord Jhesu Crist:/ this is to seyn, by delit in thynkynge, by reccheleesnesse in spekynge, and by wikked synful werkynge./ And agayns thise wikkede giltes is Penitence, that may be likned unto a tree./

The roote of this tree is Contricioun, that hideth hym in the herte of hym that is verray repentaunt, right as the roote of a tree hydeth hym in the erthe./ Of the roote of Contricioun spryngeth a stalke that bereth braunches and leves of Confessioun, and fruyt of Satisfaccioun./ For which Crist seith in his gospel: "Dooth digne fruyt of

Penitence"; for by this fruyt may men knowe this tree, and nat by the roote that is hyd in the herte of man, ne by the braunches, ne by the leves of Confessioun./ And therfore oure Lord Jhesu Crist seith thus: "By the fruyt of hem shul ye knowen hem."/ Of this roote eek spryngeth a seed of grace, the which seed is mooder of sikernesse, and this seed is egre and hoot./ The grace of this seed spryngeth of God thurgh remembrance of the day of doom and on the peynes of helle./ Of this matere seith Salomon that in the drede of God man forleteth his synne./ The heete of this seed is the love of God, and the desiryng of the joyc perdurable./ This heete draweth the herte of man to God, and dooth hym haten his synne./ For soothly ther is nothyng that savoureth so wel to a child as the milk of his norice, ne nothyng is to hym moore abhomynable than thilke milk whan it is medled with oother mete./ Right so the synful man that loveth his synne, hym semeth that it is to him moost sweete of any thyng;/ but fro that tyme that he loveth sadly oure Lord Jhesu Crist, and desireth the lif perdurable, ther nys to him no thyng moore abhomynable./ For soothly the lawe of God is the love of God; for which David the prophete seith: "I have loved thy lawe, and hated wikkednesse and hate"; he that loveth God kepeth his lawe and his word./ This tree saugh the prophete Daniel in spirit, upon the avysioun of the kyng Nabugodonosor, whan he conseiled hym to do penitence./ Penaunce is the tree of lyf to hem that it receyven, and he that holdeth hym in verray penitence is blessed, after the sentence of Salomon./

(The Canterbury Tales, X (1) 75-125)

The Cleansing of Man's Soul

MOST of the great students of Chaucer have not shared with him the doctrines and practices of his faith. For that reason most of them have found parts of his work dull and difficult which to those without their scholarship but with his faith are quite pertinent and plain. His long prose tracts are cases in point. His *Parson's Tale* is a specific example. It is mentioned without enthusiasm by most critics as a sermon on penitence and omitted as such by most readers. A study of the theory and practice of atonement for sin in an idiom technical and unfamiliar they do not find of consuming interest. That Chaucer did they do not explain. After all, it may be worth explaining.

Chaucer's prose is an honest and reliable servant, once or twice rising with the promise of an admirable Crichton into the distinction of excellent independence, but for the most part a faithful, unobtrusive purveyor for the thoughts of others. It did service to an honorable group of canonized saints: Jerome, Augustine, Gregory, Bernard; of uncanonized scholars: Aristotle, Tertullian, Seneca, Cato, Boethius. It is almost wholly translation from the works of writers such as these.

The prose works which Chaucer chose to translate are strikingly similar in subject matter; in treatise or homily or composite they deal with philosophy. More particularly they deal with ethics and metaphysics: the consolations of philosophy, the seven deadly sins, contrition, confession. This was due neither to lack nor inaccessibility of other material. There were libraries of lays and legends from which to choose; encyclopedias of stranger things than ever could be dreamed of in his philosophy; physiologies yet more wonder-filled; metaphorical mirrors and primers in plenty of the seven arts. For a man of Chaucer's mind the range was rare and magnificent. These things being so, some conclusions can be drawn regarding his persistent tastes and temper by the type of thing on which his final choice consistently lighted. Some conclusion might also be drawn on the general lassitude of readers in following him into these fields of his election. Chaucer was clearly more practically interested in the doctrine and use of the sacrament of penance than in many other matters of the day. He was more interested in it than multitudes who read him are. That is a first point to be established.

As a matter of fact, the prose tract and homily were general reading in Chaucer's time. The number of copies of *The Form of Perfect Living* that survive is one evidence. The popularity of *The Scale of Perfection* and *The Cloud of Unknowing*

is another. Spirituality was an object in life, a
practice, and an art. It could be learned; it could
be cultivated, and it should be. Books were written to inspire, to encourage, and to foster it. These
manuals of meditation were read and followed
with much the same fidelity now bestowed on
manuals of golf and bridge. Some of the most
beautiful and excellent books of this type in the
entire literature of sanctity were written in Chaucer's England during his lifetime. That very as-
tute and astounding psychological and spiritual
classic, *The Sixteen Revelations of Divine Love*,
was lived and thought and transcribed almost at
his door. He shared the spiritual life of his time.
His choice of texts for translation is part of that
magnificent sense of his age that made him so
thoroughly its master. That is a second point.

The place of the prose religious tract in the
reading world today is altered absolutely. Interest in it does not survive. Spiritual reading, which
was the delight of the leisured classes in Chaucer's
day, is now the practice of small and specialized
groups. Numbers of devout persons in secular life
read rather regularly books of religious import,
doctrinal or devotional. Such reading is the daily
practice of all men and women in religious communities. For them the continuity of religious
prose, which is an English literature in itself, has

never been broken. And for them today the *Parson's Tale* has exactly the same meaning and application and interest as it had on that hypothetical April day in 1387 that gave it literary being. For them the cleansing of man's soul is part of every day's work, and the parson's instruction on it is of immediate practical value. For them this little study may not be unwelcome.

Being a theological treatise on the sacrament of confession, the *Parson's Tale* is properly put into the mouth of a priest whose humble holiness of life is congruous with the dignity of his discourse. His popularity as a clerical model in literature is beside the point here. On lines of goodness and mortification and Christlike love, Chaucer built him into the form of Christ's disciple who, through Him, should take away the sins of the world. And to him Chaucer entrusted the discourse on the great, absolving sacrament of penance.

The treatise, in its matter, organization, and treatment, owes nothing, of course, to Chaucer except its English. Its Latin sources are generally stated; the author of the original as a compilation, if there was such a document, is not known. Its clear and methodical procedure through definition and division survives in countless books of catechetical instruction, from the catechism of the Council of Trent to the child's text today. Its plan, definitions, scriptural references, entire content, almost, are not and cannot be new. It is what may be called a standard study of penance. The style, wherever it can be, is something more than translation; for single, shining instants it is Chaucer.

The "tale" begins with a text from the prophet Jeremias and a devout comment, then a definition of the sacrament and an explanation of the times when it should be received. The exposition falls naturally into three divisions determined by the three parts of the sacrament: "Contricioun of herte, Confessioun of Mouth, and Satisfaccioun." Part I deals with the roots or reasons for contrition, the qualities of contrition, the effects of contrition, the kinds of sin, the examination of conscience, the means of avoiding sin, the seven mortal or deadly sins, with the definition, causes, and remedies for each. Part II treats of confession, the conditioning circumstances of sin, the qualities of a good confession, the manner of making a good confession. Part III discusses satisfaction to God and to one's neighbor through almsdeeds, and penance, strictly so called, prayer, fasting, mortification of one's body.

To the person who goes to confession this is, perhaps, the most familiar thing that he will find in Chaucer. He could, from memory, fill out the

subdivisions of every subject in the foregoing outline. He knows the matter, the form, the examples used. He is tremendously intrigued, to use
an out-moded word, at meeting in so classic an
environment the one practice that he felt sure he
could not share with it. All this is exactly what he
has learned in his Christian Doctrine classes, or
earlier in his little catechism. A thousand times
more than in the gardens of allegory or in the tem-
ples of courtly love he is here at home with Chaucer. He may not get a "Troilus-Cresyde" thrill out
of it, but he knows, thank God, more about the
precepts of the parson than about the pranks of
Pandar. And unless he is unusually obtuse, he will
find something of innocent delight in the Chaucerian variants of his catechism definitions of:
"Pacience" that "maketh a man lyk to God, and
maketh hym Goddes owene deere child"; of ire
that "bynymeth from man his wit and his resoun,
and al his debonaire lif espiritueel that sholde
kepen his soule"; of murmuring and complaining
"whiche wordes men clepen the develes *Pater
noster*," though the author adds simply, "the devel
ne hadde nevere *Paternoster*." He will be con-
vinced in a quaint, new manner that "oure sweete
Lord God of hevene" wills "that no man wole
perisse, but wole that we comen alle to the
knoweleche of hym, and to the blisful lif that is

perdurable." He will be touched by the disarming tenderness which describes the sinner's detestation of sin: "fro that tyme that he loveth sadly oure Lord Jhesu Crist . . . ther nys to him no thyng moore abhomynable."

Every page is a chronicle of life actual and contemporary, in all its moral phases, from sanctity to superstition. The preeminent means of sanctity then as now is the "receyvynge worthily of the precious body of Jhesu Crist," the use of the sacraments and the sacramentals, "by receyvynge eek of hooly water." The preeminent practices of superstition then as now, are by "false enchauntours," "by dremes, by chirkynge of dores, or crakkynge of houses, by gnawynge of rattes, and swich manere wrecchednesse." Between these two extremes there is a world of human conduct that a human world can share.

The whole treatise, though written in the letter of penance, is conceived in the spirit of love. And love gives it life. That life has about it a certain Chaucerian intimacy. One finds it in the devout deference of address to Christ and "his sweete Mooder"; in the profound reverence for "hooly chirche," "the sacrament of the auter," "the preciouse persone of Crist." One finds it in the repeated beautiful assurances of Christ's love for man's soul and His desire for its salvation, in summaries of redemption, and in succinct epitomes, such as this of the persons concerned in confession: "Crist is sovereyn, and the preest meene and mediatour betwixe Crist and the synnere, and the synnere is the laste by wey of resoun." One finds an equally lovely recommendation of the Pater Noster "in which orison . . . hath Jhesu Crist enclosed moost thynges." All this was, surely, written for our consolation. And for doctrine, there is, to cite one case for many, upon the subject of matrimony so pulled and hauled about both by the Canterbury crowd and their commentators, this precise and tremendous commentary: "This sacrement bitokneth the knyttynge togidre of Crist and of hooly chirche." Sin is, naturally, the major subject of the text as it is the entire matter of confession. The ease with which "skippeth venial into deedly synne" is the beguiling trap in the great human tragedy. The parson makes that all quite plain. His model and his language could have once been met in Galilee.

But the sacrament of penance is, most of all, the glorious *deus ex machina* to avert possible final disaster, to catch up life and death into a divine, deific comedy. Humanity, which it is bound on saving, is a blunderer. Penance takes it usually in the act or the acknowledgment of its most blind or foul or perverse blunders. The situations are bound to be unflattering and a little ludicrous. They can be comic. The treatise bristles with instances. The proud man appears, fussing for precedence in the giving of the kiss of peace, the "kisse pax," a ceremony which, on the gravest occasions, can often be, humanly, very funny. The sinner is told that all the good he does while in the state of mortal sin is absolutely without merit in God's sight. Of all possible examples to illustrate the point, what should serve so well as the popular song of the hour: "Wel may that man . . . synge thilke newe Frenshe song, 'Jay tout perdu mon temps et mon labour.'" Never was doctrine more amusingly defended by a ditty. It is about the most deliciously funny thing in Chaucer. It may possibly point to a French original of the "tale." It sounds much more like Chaucer's quick-witted, pertinent impertinence, contributed out of the current hit of the season. The perennial habit of deploring the present in terms of the past exercises itself in the matter of "the synful costlewe array of wommen." As for the confusion resulting from their "lording it" over mere men, the parson says: "Ther neden none ensamples of this; the experience of day by day oghte suffise." It was little enough for all that so good a priest might have wished to say, that day, to the wife of Bath.

Only those who go to confession know the multitudes of humorous possibilities there can be in the most devout and reverent use of the sacrament. Those who believe neither in sin nor its forgiveness naturally cannot see anything to laugh at in the situation. The parson saw it from two sides, both of them very human, both of them amusing in spots. He has left his comments as a little legacy to the laughter of the world.

His advice to penitents has a canny humor and a keen kindliness. "Thow shalt nat eek peynte thy confessioun by faire subtile wordes," he says, "for thanne bigilestow thyself, and nat the preest. Thow most tellen it platly, be it nevere so foul ne so horrible." He knows thoroughly the inclination to leave "olde confessours" and instructs the penitent to tell all his sins to the same confessor, "and nat a parcel to o man and a parcel to another." This is, he observes, "nys but stranglynge of thy soule." The profound business of sanctification with which penance is concerned he kept in the very front of his thought. He says: "Thow shalt eek shryve thee to a preest that is discreet to conseille thee"; an implied comment on tales told in the way. The whole temper of the treatise is indicated in his simple statement that the sinner "is unkynde to Crist" who "certes is moore strong for to unbynde than synne is strong for to bynde."

This, briefly, is the summary of the *Parson's Tale* with some simple illustrations of the matter of the old Latin treatise in the tongue of Chaucer. It is not without human interest, not without spiritual beauty, not without humor. Chaucer cared for it enough to give his time to it. It is possibly the least read of his works. There is this much to be said in protest. Confession is the greatest of all solutions for the greatest of all human needs. It deals with the very stuff of life; more particularly, the stuff of sin and its occasions. It has these in common with the world's great classics. Psychologically it is the sanest way to peace, if not to pardon. A thoroughly sane and correct exposition of it, on a human and normal level, has as much to recommend it as contemporary publications on spontaneous confessions and shared soul-experiences. In this day of disclosures the truth about confession from Chaucer ought to have considerable vogue.

A Child's Book of Stars

A Treatise on the Astrolabe

LYTE LOWYS my sone, I aperceyve wel by certeyne evydences thyn abilite to lerne sciences
touching nombres and proporciouns; and as wel
considre I thy besy praier in special to lerne the
tretys of the Astrelabie. Than for as mochel as a
philosofre saith, "he wrappith him in his frend,
that condescendith to the rightfulle praiers of his
frend," therfore have I yeven the a suffisant Astrolabie as for oure orizonte, compowned after the
latitude of Oxenforde; upon which, by media-
cioun of this litel tretys, I purpose to teche the a
certein nombre of conclusions aperteynyng to the
same instrument. I seie a certein of conclusions,
for thre causes. The first cause is this: truste wel
that alle the conclusions that han be founde, or
ellys possibly might be founde in so noble an instrument as is an Astrelabie ben unknowe parfitly
to eny mortal man in this regioun, as I suppose.
Another cause is this, that sothly in any tretis of
the Astrelabie that I have seyn there be somme conclusions that wol not in alle thinges parformen
her bihestes; and somme of hem ben to harde to
thy tendir age of ten yeer to conceyve.

This tretis, divided in 5 parties, wol I shewe the
under full light reules and naked wordes in Englissh, for Latyn ne canst thou yit but small, my

litel sone. But natheles suffise to the these trewe conclusions in Englissh as wel as sufficith to these noble clerkes Grekes these same conclusions in Grek; and to Arabiens in Arabik, and to Jews in Ebrew, and to the Latyn folk in Latyn; whiche Latyn folk had hem first out of othere dyverse langages, and writen hem in her owne tunge, that is to seyn, in Latyn. And God woot that in alle these langages and in many moo han these conclusions ben suffisantly lerned and taught, and yit by diverse reules; right as diverse pathes leden diverse folk the righte way to Rome. Now wol I preie mekely every discret persone that redith or herith this litel tretys to have my rude endityng for excusid, and my superfluite of wordes, for two causes. The first cause is for that curious endityng and hard sentence is ful hevy at onys for such a child to lerne. And the secunde cause is this, that sothly me semith better to writen unto a child twyes a god sentence, than he forgete it onys.

And Lowys, yf so be that I shewe the in my light Englissh as trewe conclusions touching this mater, and not oonly as trewe but as many and as subtile conclusiouns, as ben shewid in Latyn in eny commune tretys of the Astrelabie, konne me the more thank. And preie God save the king, that is lord of this langage, and alle that him feith berith and obeieth, everich in his degre, the more

and the lasse. But considre wel that I ne usurpe
not to have founden this werk of my labour or of
myn engyn. I n'am but a lewd compilator of the
labour of olde astrologiens, and have it translatid
in myn Englissh oonly for thy doctrine. And with
this swerd shal I sleen envie.

Prima pars.—The firste partie of this tretys shal
reherse the figures and the membres of thyn Astrelabie by cause that thou shalt have the gretter
knowing of thyn owne instrument.

Secunda pars.—The secunde partie shal techen
the worken the verrey practik of the forseide conclusiouns, as ferforth and as narwe as may be
shewed in so small an instrument portatif aboute.
For wel woot every astrologien that smallist fraccions ne wol not be shewid in so small an instrument as in subtile tables calculed for a cause.

Tertia pars.—The thirde partie shal contene
diverse tables of longitudes and latitudes of
sterres fixe for the Astrelabie, and tables of the
declinacions of the sonne, and tables of longitudes
of citees and townes; and tables as well for the
governaunce of a clokke, as for to fynde the altitude meridian; and many anothir notable conclusioun after the kalenders of the reverent clerkes,
Frere J. Somer and Frere N. Lenne.

Quarta pars.—The fourthe partie shal ben a
theorike to declare the moevyng of the celestiall

bodies with the causes. The whiche fourthe partie in speciall shal shewen a table of the verrey moeving of the mone from houre to houre every day and in every signe after thyn almenak. Upon which table there folewith a canoun suffisant to teche as wel the manere of the worchynge of the same conclusioun as to knowe in oure orizonte with which degre of the zodiak that the mone arisith in any latitude, and the arisying of any planete after his latitude fro the ecliptik lyne.

Quinta pars.—The fifthe partie shal be an introductorie, after the statutes of oure doctours, in which thou maist lerne a gret part of the generall rewles of theorik in astrologie. In which fifthe partie shalt thou fynden tables of equaciouns of houses after the latitude of Oxenforde; and tables of dignitees of planetes, and othere notefull thinges, yf God wol vouche saaf and his Moder the Maide, moo then I behete.

(*A Treatise on the Astrolabe,* Introduction)

A Child's Book of Stars

A TEXT BOOK in astronomy for children is fairly rare today. A treatise in astronomy written by a father for his small son is even rarer. Fathers and sons are not now sufficiently interested in the firmament to inspire and support publications of this sort. Chaucer, in his very final forties, sat down and wrote such a book for his ten year old boy, Lewis. There is something pleasanter than a pun in the fact that "the oldest work . . . in English upon the scientific instrument for measuring the stars" was written by the "morning star of English song." Parents and teachers may like to remember this of him. They do not read the book. The same partial devotion to Chaucer that dismisses the *Treatise on the Astrolabe* because it is a translation dedicates itself to *The Romaunt of the Rose* although it is a closer translation. Also, it would seem that to the modern reader, the science of astronomy is less familiar than the science of Venus. The luster of a living solar system has faded, in this day of research, before the dead moon of courtly love. But the reader who both loves and respects Chaucer will meet him on this uncommon common ground of childhood and the stars.

His *Treatise on the Astrolabe,* so consistently

neglected even by scholars, is an easy approach to him. Like the *Complete Angler* it is a picture of the author's disposition, the recreation that he made of his recreation. It is an unmistakable avowal of one splendid Chaucerian pastime, a unique study of father and son, and altogether a satisfactory modern or medieval text book. These aspects of the treatise are worth considering.

Chaucer was always a busy man. In 1391, as Clerk of the King's Works, he was occupied with the construction and supervision of roads between Greenwich and Woolwich. He was more creatively and pleasurably engaged in the construction and supervision of a classic literary highway between London and Canterbury. He was at work on the *Prologue* and the first of the *Canterbury Tales*. Obviously, he had enough to do. That he wrote, at this time, a treatise on astronomy is evidence of his conviction that it was worth doing. The translating and compiling of a scientific treatise out of Latin originals does not suggest itself, save for very special reasons, as an irresistible alternative. Chaucer had three special, perfect reasons. His boy had asked him for a book about the stars in English, easy enough for him to read; the lad had an evident aptitude for mathematical sciences; the books accessible to him were too hard. These are Chaucer's reasons for writing the

Astrolabe; they may even appeal to some as reasons for reading it.

The treatise brings one face to face with a father, with his pastime, his hobby and his son to share it. Chaucer liked astronomy. Books on the subject were in his home, Latin texts and adaptations from the Greek and Arabic and Hebrew. He knew the use of the astrolabe, that intricate, medieval instrument for measuring the stars. He had worked with the more complicated instruments and had at least a small one in his home. These absorbing books, this fascinating, star-taking instrument had teased beyond endurance the curiosity of the small Lewis with his "litel Latyn." Repeatedly he had begged his father to explain them to him. Chaucer got the boy a little instrument for himself, "thyn Astrelabie." He translated and simplified one of the most practical Latin volumes. He may have called it *Bread and Milk for Children*; he did call it *Treatise on the Astrolabie*. Of all facts and conjectures upon the domestic life of Chaucer, these are among the happiest.

Without assuming or aspiring to completeness in the science of the stars, he made of it a thoroughly painstaking and experimental pastime. With much more than a dilettante's enthusiasm he read and studied and worked out problems for his own locality, the latitude of Oxford. With the sheer earnestness of a lover of science, albeit an amateur, he experimented with his "nobil" instrument upon many of the practically numberless computations possible even in one vicinity. With Ptolemy, no less than Dante, he walked among the stars. His treatise bears abundant evidence of consistent, careful statement of his problem, skill and ingenuity in handling equipment, precision in method and observation, controlled judgment and that aloof, cool honesty which marks the scientific mind. Withal, it glows with a quiet incandescence of enthusiasm by which even translation becomes illustrious. *"To knowe,"* he says, *"the altitude of the sonne or of othre celestial bodies.* Put the ryng of thyn Astrelabie upon thy right thombe, and turne thi lift syde ageyn the light of the sonne."* Here is the man, careful even with his play, competent even with his child's plaything. Or again, "Tak a round plate of metal; for werpyng, the brodder the better. . . . And in the centre of the compas styke an evene pyn, or a wyr, upright, the smaller the better." He sees through his apparatus to his principle and can improvise equipment to meet a need, if need be. He is wary of generalizations or unwarranted assumptions; "natheles this rule in generall wol I warne the for evere." And for a perfect picture of Chau-

cer at work in his home laboratory one has only
to dramatize such a bit as: "by experience I wot
wel that in our orisounte . . . in taking of a just
ascendent in a portatif Astrelabie it is hard to
knowe." The portable model sounds thoroughly
contemporary. One loves to watch him through
the ardent enthusiasm of his text: "Than tok I a
subtil compas," "Than leide I down softly my
compas," "And now is my sonne gon to reste."
And one is thoroughly ready to study stars on such
an invitation as: "Yf thou wilt pleye this craft
with the arisyng of the mone, loke thou rekne
wel hir cours houre by houre." This is a very pattern of a "compleat angler" in the deep pools of
the sky, a fourteenth century Walton of the stars.

It would be a welcome work of supererogation
to multiply examples, to gather gay handfuls of
evidence of Chaucer's joy in his happy craft, his
competence and enthusiasm in his pastime. These
few instances will serve for many and leave no
question of the nature and degree of Chaucer's
skill as an amateur astronomer, of the kind and
quality of his recreation. Even in the intoxication
of an English May or on the merry way to Canterbury, it is pleasant to watch him compassing life
between two crepuscules or finding shining pastime with the spheres.

It is pleasanter, even, to watch the fine com-

panionship in which father and son share their
hobby of the heavens. The book beautifully knits
up the lives of the two. It begins with a preface
that makes luminous even a treatise on the sun.
"Lyte Lowys my sone,"—with this key of delicate
endearment he opens his child's wonder-box of
stars. And then a key of parental pride he turns:
"I aperceyve wel by certeyne evydences thyn abilite to lerne sciences touching nombres and proporciouns," and then this golden third: "and as
wel considre I thy besy praier in special to lerne
the tretys of the Astrelabie." Something more en-
during than the stars shines out from Chaucer's
mind in this line, that tremendous paternity of
his heart whose pattern is deific. Comment on the
loveliness of mutual relationship between this
mediaeval father and his son would be imperti-
nent. The father himself invests it with a dual,
double dignity: "he wrappith him in his frend,
that condescendith to the rightfulle praiers of his
frend." One understands in Chaucer something
beyond a precocious application of a classic text
when he calls his child his friend.

With beautiful ease he has lifted the child to
his level. Straightway he makes him entirely com-
fortable there. He does not strain or push him
beyond his mental capacities. This little book
is to be entirely within his understanding. Ex-

pressly to this end certain "conclusions" have been omitted because they "ben to harde to thy tendir age of ten yeer to conceyve." Not only the difficulty of complicated problems but the child's limited vocabulary in English and more limited one in Latin the father keeps in mind. So the maker of English sets himself to speak the language of childhood. "This tretis . . . wol I shewe the under full light reules and naked wordes in Englissh, for Latyn ne canst thou yit but small, my litel sone." The sentence is a smile and a caress. The boy is, however, to understand both the excellence of the treatise made to his order, as also the gratitude with which he should receive it. These two matters his father puts quite directly before him. "Lowys, yf so be that I shewe the in my light English as trewe conclusions . . . and not oonly as trewe but as many and as subtile conclusiouns, as ben shewid in Latyn in eny commune tretys . . . konne me the more thank." And however much his aspiration, "preie God save the king" may have been a matter of convention and habit, it was a good Chaucerian habit of loyalty long sustained.

Less precedented than this lesson in patriotism is his fine lesson in professional honesty. The lad is not to rate him too highly, is not to think him more learned than he is. He is to understand clearly that his father neither discovered nor de-veloped any of the scientific principles that he is giving him in simple form. The ground is cut clean from under any possible disillusionment in later days. Chaucer will keep, of all things, the respect of his son. "Considre wel that I ne usurpe not to have founden this werk of my labour or of myn engyn," he says to the boy, and then with not entirely unmixed motives to a less generous audience: "I n'am but a lewd compilator of the labour of olde astrologiens, and have it translatid in myn Englissh oonly for thy doctrine. And with this swerd shall I sleen envie." The sentence leaps out of the text with sudden, fierce vindictiveness, quells malice with a gesture and falls laughing back into the context, a shining blade of truth beside its happy sheath of humor. Nothing could be more typically Chaucerian. Packed with an all but incongruous concentrate of humility and canniness and candor, his apology honors the boy to whom it is addressed and puts into instant practice the simplest of all ideals of professional ethics in a day when plagiarism was a custom and not a crime.

The relations between Chaucer and his little Lewis throughout the *Astrolabe* are never more touching than as father and son, never more dignified than as friend and friend, and never more positive than as teacher and pupil. It was upon the effectiveness of this relation that the success of the book, at the moment, depended. It was probably the hardest of all relations to maintain. But present through the text is a persuasively preceptorial manner, tempered always to the child's ability, by which the devoted father is no less the thorough teacher. One recognizes the successful compromise between fondness and firmness in "Forget not thys, litel Lowys," "Now have I told the twyes," "Understond wel," and again "forget it not." One reads these with a curious sense of nearness to Chaucer, a feeling that here one is close to the man who was an unusual father and an unusual teacher to his child. His immense gift to literature is quite forgotten for the moment in the presence of a gift more human, almost more divine.

His capacities as a teacher are manifest not only in his pupil but in his text. The *Astrolabe*, for all its precious autobiography, is quite perfect as a text. It may somewhat disconcert educators today to find a fourteenth century controller of customs in possession of a perfect theory and practice of teaching. It may amaze them to find a builder of roads supervising highways to the sun. Both his theory and his practice are worth imitating. On a subject beset with possibilities of child rimes he did not write a translation and elaboration of

"*Mica, mica, parva stella*" for his boy. In the very heaven and household of stellified myths he did not write a mythology. He did not for a moment deceive his pupil into thinking that he was playing with a puzzle or puzzling with a plaything. He did not even try to give his book an easy or attractive name. *Bread and Milk for Children* it is called in some manuscripts, but in his text it was the "*Astrelabie.*" Lewis was not tricked or trapped into a difficult study by a cunning snare of title. He was curiously unhampered in getting straight to the stars.

The book, though incomplete, is a model of order and organization, divided, as the author says in the introduction, "in 5 parties." They are: an explanation of the mechanism of the astrolabe, its working, tables of longitude and time, the orbits of celestial bodies, an introduction into the theory of astrology. It is a manual for experiment as well and Lewis is studying, in modern idiom, a laboratory science. He had his own portable astrolabe. The little instrument, his father-teacher reminds him, will not show the "smallist fraccions" of the more "subtile tables." The picture of this little fourteenth century boy of ten at work with his "smal . . . instrument portatif" forms a subject of thoughtful contemplation for teachers and students in over-equipped laboratories today. Proper acknowledgment is made of sources, direct and indirect, from the "noble clerkes Grekes" to the more contemporary compilers of calendars, the "reverent clerkes, Frere J. Somer and Frere N. Lenne."

The text proper proceeds in paragraph after paragraph of clear, direct, and easy exposition, emphasized occasionally by repetition, illustrated always by example and sometimes by small diagrams. Rather gratuitously the author prays "mekely every discret persone that redith" his treatise to excuse his "rude endityng" and his "superfluite of wordes" for the two sound reasons that "curious endityng and hard sentence is ful hevy at onys for such a child to lerne. And . . . me semith better to writen unto a child twyes a god sentence, than he forgete it onys." This sentence in itself establishes both the quality of the book as a text and the competence of the author as a teacher.

One problem after another he states and solves in the most specific way. "The yeer of oure Lord 1391, the 12 day of March at midday, I wolde knowe the degre of the sonne." The method in itself sounds inexorable, were it not illuminated by such instructions in the manual as "Take than thin Astrelabie . . . so that thou worke softly and avysely" or "to prove this conclusioun . . . thou must have a plomet hangyng on a lyne, heygher than thin heved, on a perche." Perhaps best of all is this example where the mere loveliness of the statement holds compensation for the sacrifice of sleep: "In som wynters nyght whan the firmament is cler and thikke sterred, wayte a tyme til that eny sterre fix sitte lyne-right perpendiculer over the pool artik . . . Tak than . . . the altitude of A . . . and forget it not, let A and F goo fare wel tyl ageynst the dawenyng a gret while, and com than ageyn." Even as a proposition, one is glad to think that this was not too big and beautiful for Lewis Chaucer.

Nowhere does the *Astrolabe* suffer the constraints of a literal translation; nowhere does it betray the Latinity of its origin. Occasionally through the easy, facile flow of the teacher's exposition thrills the quiet beauty of the poet's prose. "Among an heep of sterres fixe it liked me for to take the altitude of the faire white sterre that is clepid Alhabor." Occasionally one hears the music of the spheres as here: "the houre of Mercurie entring under my west orizonte at eve . . . and so furth by ordir, planete after planete in houre after houre, all the nyght longe til the sonne arise." On such a night, one feels, science and poetry had met and kissed.

After all, the test of a text is pragmatic. One

cannot know how well Chaucer's *Astrolabe* suc-
ceeded as such in its day. And it is not probable
that it will be adopted in elementary schools immediately. But the ten year old boy today plays
with toys as complicated and expensive as the astrolabe of Lewis Chaucer. It would be interesting
to put into his hands a duplicate of that little instrument and a modernized copy of the text with
a competent instructor. Teachers might begin
teaching Chaucer to children. They have tried
projects less commendable.

All that has here been said of this particular
work of Chaucer might easily remain unsaid as of
the merest relative importance. Two sentences in
the *Astrolabe* stand, in his collected work, as of
absolute importance, two declarations, one of orthodoxy, one of love. In the days of dark arts,
astrology was frequently black and not always
beautiful. Chaucer knew its heights and depths.
He loved its heights with ardor; he dismissed its
spurious abuses with deep disdain. He would have
nothing of even the least offensive practices. It
was, at the time, a rather nice test of orthodox
Christianity. "These ben . . . rytes of payens, in
whiche my spirit hath no feith," he says. Not with
magicians but with magi did he follow the stars.

At the end of that loveliest piece of prose he
ever wrote, the introduction to the *Astrolabe*, he

projects his little work under the glory of this condition: "if God wol vouche saaf and his Moder the Maide." Faith alone might well have employed the language of doctrine; Chaucer might have written "the blessed Virgin" or "the Virgin Mary." That would have expressed faith, but not the mighty splendor of his love. For in the very zenith of his heavens shone the sign of a Woman wearing the sun, moonshod and crowned with stars. She is God's and his Mother, the Maid.

Research is fond of reconstructing portraits of Chaucer from epithets and phrases dropped among his books. When all such quests are ended there will still be the pictures of these two at work with their astrolabe through the quiet evenings in the home in Kent, Chaucer and his little Lewis and their child's book of stars.

The Chaucer Canon

Here Taketh the Makere of this Book His Leve

Now preye I to hem alle that herkne this litel tretys or rede, that if ther be any thyng in it that liketh hem, that therof they thanken oure Lord Jhesu Crist, of whom procedeth al wit and al goodnesse./ And if ther be any thyng that displese hem, I preye hem also that they arrette it to the dcfaute of myn unkonnynge, and nat to my wyl, that wolde ful fayn have seyd bettre if I hadde had konnynge./ For oure book seith, "Al that is writen is writen for oure doctrine," and that is myn en-tente./ Wherfore I biseke yow mekely, for the mercy of God, that ye preye for me that Crist have mercy on me and foryeve me my giltes;/ and namely of my translacions and enditynges of worldly vanitees, the whiche I revoke in my re-tracciouns;/ as is the book of Troilus; the book also of Fame; the book of the xix Ladies; the book of the Duchesse; the book of Seint Valentynes day of the Parlement of Briddes; the tales of Caunter-bury, thilke that sownen into synne;/ the book of the Leoun; and many another book, if they were in my remembrance, and many a song and many a leccherous lay; that Crist for his grete mercy foryeve me the synne./ But of the translacion of Boece de Consolacione, and othere bookes of legendes of seintes, and omelies, and moralitee, and devocioun,/ that thanke I oure Lord Jhesu Crist and his blisful Mooder, and alle the seintes of hevene,/ bisekynge hem that they from hennes forth unto my lyves ende sende me grace to biwayle my giltes, and to studie to the salvacioun of my soule, and graunte me grace of verray penitence, confessioun and satisfaccioun to doon in this present lyf,/ thurgh the benigne grace of hym that is kynge of kynges and preest over alle preestes, that boghte us with the precious blood of his herte;/ so that I may been oon of hem at the day of doom that shulle be saved. *Qui cum patre et Spiritu Sancto vivit et regnat Deus per omnia secula. Amen.*

Heere is ended the book of the tales of Caunterbury, compiled by Geffrey Chaucer, of whos soule Jhesu Crist have mercy. Amen.

(*The Canterbury Tales,* X (1) 1081-1092)

The Chaucer Canon

THE most devastating criticism ever written of Chaucer was written by himself. The most rigorous censorship exercised at any time upon his work was that which he exercised. The most thorough expurgation of his books was his own. After thirty years and more of spontaneous, joyous, racy writing for the most part of a very human kind, he unwrote, by will and in a single sentence, a good third of all his work. It was, for him, probably the most important sentence that he ever wrote, his composite act of contrition, confession, and amendment. He called it his "retracciouns." It appears after the *Parson's Tale* at the end of the *Canterbury Tales*. The sentence is:

"Wherfore I biseke yow mekely, for the mercy of God, that ye preye for me that Crist have mercy on me and foryeve me my giltes; and namely of my translacions and enditynges of world vanitees, the whiche I revoke in my rctracciouns; as is the book of Troilus; the book also of Fame; the book of the .xix. Ladies; the book of the Duchesse; the book of Seint Valentynes day of the Parlement of Briddes; the tales of Canterbury, thilke that sownen into synne; the book of the Leoun; and many another book, if they were in my remembrance, and many a song and many a leccherous lay; that Crist for his grete mercy foryeve me the synne."

In making this categorically inclusive revocation Chaucer was suffering neither from scruples nor the qualms of a death-bed repentance, as is sometimes supposed. He was following in time, it is true, the examples of great penitents and converts and scholars. He had for precedent, had that been necessary, men like St. Jerome and St. Augustine and Boccaccio. But like them, he was conforming to the teachings of the Church in that one supreme matter for which the Church existed for him, the salvation of his soul. Penance was the normal, sacramental means provided by the Church for that end. The essentials of the sacrament he well understood; through the mouth of his parson he had enumerated them in his great discourse on Penitence: "verray perfit Penitence . . . stant on three thynges: Contricioun of herte, Confessioun of Mouth, and Satisfaccioun." His retractation is the fulfillment of these three conditions.

Chaucer, being a Catholic, went to confession. His own counsel is "generally, shryve thee ofte." This is much more than saying that Chaucer went to Flanders or France or Italy. The matter and the manner of his work came in part from the continent but its final moral evaluation came from

confession. He had almost a theological acquaint-
ance with the qualities of a good confession. He
had translated an admirable treatise on it. He
knew that a penitent, to obtain absolution for his
sins, must repent of them with a sorrow universal,
sovereign, and entire. That contrition involved a
detestation of one's own specific sins, "sorweful
bitternesse of herte" and a firm purpose of amendment; "soothly he ne sholde nat thanne in all his
lyf have corage to synne, but yeven his body and al
his herte to the service of Jhesu Crist." Sorrow
for sin, for the Catholic, is not a term of vague
general inclusiveness. It is a specific act of effec-
tive regret for all the specific offenses against the
law of God of which he knows himself to be guilty.
He arrives at this knowledge of his guilt usually
with the aid of a more or less detailed table of
sins or examination of conscience included in or-
dinary prayer books. Chaucer has such an outline
in the second part of the *Parson's Tale*. It involves
the review and evaluation of all one's thoughts,
words, acts as morally good or bad. However difficult the theory may sound, the practice is familiar
to most Catholic children of seven. After contrition, it is one's immediate preparation for confession.

For Chaucer this meant that he must examine
his writings, not as adequate translations, nor as

delicate poetry, nor as consummate narrative art, but as moral acts. It was as such that God regarded and judged them, and as such that he would be responsible for them. Anyone who has ever examined his conscience honestly and made a sincere confession knows Chaucer's position. What he cannot share with him is the experience of having the authorship of a small shelf of English classics as subject of examination and of having the creation of world literature as matter of confession. With a sort of savage earnestness Chaucer examined his writer's soul, made of his collected works matters of conscience, to speak in the idiom of penance. He was not now concerned with the stuff of literature but with the stuff of sanctity; he was not disquieted over the loss of a pagan lover but over the jeopardy of a Christian soul; he was not qualifying for the court of Venus but for the kingdom of heaven. He was about the divine and paradoxical business of losing his life to find it. Nothing mattered quite so much to him as God's pardon and the "blissful lif" with "oure sweete Lord God of hevene." The occasion was not without humor. Chaucer knew it well. Earlier he had written: "For soothly oure sweete Lord Jhesu Crist hath spared us so debonnairly in oure folies, that if he ne hadde pitee of mannes soule, a sory song we myghten alle synge."

The norm by which he tested his work was the

bluntest, least compromising of critical principles
and the first one, often, to be ignored, the simple
test of moral goodness or badness. Not the nice-
ness of Aristotelian proportion, not the story for
the story's sake, not emotion nor truth in terms of
beauty, not significant form mattered to him so
much as that. He knew emotion and had lived it
in vicarious lives aplenty; truth he loved and gar-
mented in raiment of never-so-alluring beauty;
and literary form got much of its significance from
his informing thought. All these were considera-
tions but not the prime, essential one. Even his
good mediaeval principles of rhetoric did not di-
vert him. All his "slye wey," his almost jaunty ease
of style by which digression, amplification, and
the whole devious machinery of delay became
more a delight than a device, were set aside with
the impersonal resolution. Dante in the *Inferno*
was less ruthless. He remembered there his own
good style. But Chaucer is single-minded and cate-
gorical and unemotional. His books morally are
either good or bad. The bad he will banish, those
translations and editings of worldly vanities that
smack of sin. The good he thanks God for and His
most blessed Mother.

After the examination of conscience and the
oral confession there still remains for the penitent
the obligation of amendment. This, in cases of

scandal or flagrant bad example, requires a retraction or revocation, so far as possible, of the causes of offense to others. It is practically the only way to counteract, in any degree, the effects of the written word. Chaucer's retractation is clearly such a moral document, an evidence not only that he went to confession but that he fulfilled to the last detail, the requirements of the sacrament. Of his complete sincerity there can be no question. Few penitents have left more convincing proofs; few have been less compromising, less apologetic. Few have made more practical effort to counteract so far as is reasonably possible, their influence upon others.

All of this, to the modern critic, sounds frightfully old-fashioned and stupidly pious and something of an affront to art, whatever that may be. In anyone less chronically normal and robust than Chaucer it could be taken to indicate any of a nice choice and variety of complexes. The thing is too unmistakably clear-headed and intentional and deliberate to be taken for anything but what it is. Indeed, the sanest scholarship sees no reason for questioning either its genuineness or its purpose. The *Retractation* is strictly a moral evaluation, having nothing at all to say of literary qualities or excellencies. As such it furnishes the reader

with Chaucer's own canon of approved and rejected books.

Nothing could be more simply devout than the
statement of his retraction. Nothing could be more
astounding than its scope. With his first word he
unwrites, morally, his *Troilus and Cresyde,* the
first English novel. More than Cresyde by faithlessness or Troilus by despair, he undoes these death-
less two. Something of the magnificence of his
narrative art in the book Chaucer surely knew;
something, also, of the subtle fineness of the characters as creations, but his close-ups of Cresyde
had troubled him, even more surely. He had re-
gretted them in the *Legend of Good Women.* She
lamented the faithlessness behind them with all
the futility of her practical and glamorous insta-
bility. The entire book, however alluring, stands
as a protest against false love. It ends with an
apostrophe to its young readers, anathematizing
false and pagan "corsed old rites" and raising high
the figure of Christ crucified for worship and true
love. Yet, at its core, it is an exposition of courtly
love, pagan, not morally justifiable, and therefore
not justified by Chaucer.

His reasons for revoking the *House of Fame*
are less grave; indeed, its preoccupation with af-
fairs of the world, fame, and "Loves folk" form
the sum of its offending. From a religious point of

view the poem might be characterized as worldly; it is not devotional, not positively concerned with spirituality and therefore not to the author's moral credit. His made-to-order martyrology of Cupid's saints, the *Legend of Good Women,* though pagan in theme, was even less offensive, less interesting, and probably eliminated by Chaucer with less regret. Except that the *Book of the Duchess* is based on a composite of pagan myth and love-vision convention there seems small reason for its rejection on moral grounds. The noisy fun of the *Parliament of Fowls,* its keen political and social satire, and the ruthless give and take on the subject of courtly love are all thoroughly worldly and so outside the Chaucer canon of approved books. Of the lost *Book of the Lion* there is, of course, nothing to be said.

In the *Canterbury Tales,* reasons for remorse and revocations are fairly obvious. Manners, no less than morality, suggest a number: the *Miller's,* the *Reeve's,* the *Summoner's,* the *Merchant's.* Chaucer's explicit eliminations offer scant hope of survival to various other pilgrims and their wares. The Wife of Bath would undoubtedly have gone the way of Cresyde and Love's martyrs, also the pardoner with his brazen sacrileges and fierce, deliberate defiance of death, and lesser offenders in kind or in degree.

There are plenty to protest at this oblation of literary perfection to moral goodness, many to argue with Chaucer over the rigor of his canon, their reasons as against his being almost as old and ultimately not quite so good. But at bottom there is no quarrel; they proclaim an artistic value which is present; he announces a spiritual value which is absent. Among everything that he had written he chose out such works as, having a supernatural motive, would entitle him to a supernatural reward. All else he rejected in balancing accounts with God, in attending to the business of saving his soul. His rejections have been duly reviewed and may be dismissed.

The books to which he attaches supernatural merit and for which he thanks God are: "the translacion of Boece de Consolacione, and othere bookes of legendes of seintes, and omelies, and moralitee, and devocioun." For these he says expressly "thanke I oure Lord Jhesu Crist and his blisful Mooder, and alle the seintes of hevene."

His *Boece* is his longest prose translation, tremendously important as a philosophical training and as a source of many of his metaphysical and moral notions. Neither his recommendation nor the excellence of the work itself has popularized it. Generally one does not read the *Consolations of Philosophy*. Generally one does not read Boccaccio's commentary on the *Divine Comedy*. Which is one way of stating that the average reader is only average. The saints' legends to which Chaucer refers are, of course, the prioress's lovely story of little Hugh of Lincoln and the second nun's life of St. Cecilia in the *Canterbury Tales*. The *Physician's Tale* of the daughter of Virginius and the *Man of Law's* longer story of Dame Custance are exemplary enough in subject and treatment to approximate the saint's legend class. Chaucer's own discourse on patience in *Tale of Melibee* and the *Parson's* treatise on penitence are both homeletic expositions of "moralitee." And for devotion, one has his A.B.C. which, however, whenever written, is his love song to his Queen.

This, then, is the Chaucer canon. In its narrowest limitations it includes only what is generally regarded as least interesting, least excellent, least Chaucerian in Chaucer. Applied in the letter still but with the greatest possible margin of that letter, it can include everything except what is rejected by name, it can include the best certainly and most of the greatest of his work.

The *Retractation* establishes two facts about him: first, that he regarded the morality of a work its essential quality; secondly, he wished to let his own work live or die by that principle. Aesthetics has this straightforward lesson to learn from him.

Critics might profitably meditate somewhat on it. Readers might be guided by it.

Its position in his manuscripts at the end of a treatise on penitence, and its position in time, almost at the end of his life, though he could not have known that, give it the force of something beyond a convention. Or, if a convention, it need not, for that reason, be insincere. The multitudinous conventional withdrawals and acknowledgments current among writers today and yesterday are as honest as most things that get into print. That was probably true also in the fourteenth century. The quiet gesture by which Chaucer annihilated, in will, the master-works of his craft and art is not so amazing, all things considered. It was neither melodrama nor scruples. It was the outward sign of faith and hope and love, the theological three, and of his moral responsibility to them. It was a grim determined stride to a heavenly Jerusalem. He might have been content with the immortality of a pilgrim. He desired the immortality of a penitent. He had reached Canterbury; he would reach Christ.

O Yonge, Fresshe Folkes

O Yonge, Fresshe Folkes

THE story of Troilus and Criseyde was old before Chaucer was born. It is young and new and perennial as the discovery of young love, the heights of its apotheosis, the depths of its betrayal. Since it was in the air in Chaucer's day, he as a consummate story-teller, could not have missed sleeping over it, dreaming over it, and then retelling it. This he did with the very perfection of his art. This he did, too, in the setting and with the elaborated conventions of courtly love. The unimportance and artificiality of these fall away in the presence of the essential tragedy, and what Thomas Campbell has called "its almost desolate simplicity." That aspect, that quality of Chaucer's *Troilus and Criseyde* may be worth brief consideration. His commentary on it to the youth of his day deserves even more consideration.

Stripped to this starkness the story runs thus. The Trojan war, that most romantic of world wars, is coming to its catastrophic end. Calkas, "a lord of gret auctorite," a diviner and an expert in contemporary science, foreseeing the fall of Troy, leaves the city and allies himself to the Greeks. The pattern is unhappily familiar. He climaxes his treachery by leaving his daughter, Criseyde, beautiful, young, a widow, to shift for herself in the soldier-ridden town.

On a day as he marches with his young knights past the temple of Venus, Troilus catches sight of the lovely girl entering its portals. Now Troilus is the bravest of the sons of King Priam, save only Hector. Moreover, he is perhaps the most eligible bachelor in Troy and the least accessible. His impervious detachment, however, collapses at the sight of Criseyde. His love for her, immediate and overwhelming, follows all the conventions, details, detours of courtly love.

Pandarus, the hyper-efficient uncle of Criseyde, arranges not one, but many meetings for Troilus with his niece. Troths are plighted, vows exchanged, and Troilus becomes the true love and the liege knight of Criseyde. Days of bewildering happiness follow.

Meanwhile, the war goes on. Calkas, in the security of the Greek sector, bethinks himself of his daughter and arranges for her transfer to him.

> Whi trowe ye my fader in this wise
> Coveyteth so to se me, but for drede
> Lest in this town that folkes me despise
> Because of hym, for his unhappy dede?

she asks naively, and promises to return to her love "er dayes ten." Troilus, stricken and shattered, provides her with a noble military escort out to the gates of the city.

And therwithal he moste his leve take,
And caste his eye upon hire pitously,
And neer he rood, his cause for to make,
To take hire by the hande al sobrely.
And Lord! so she gan wepen tendrely!

His parting is not made easier by the fact that
Diomede, the Greek, has been waiting since dawn
to meet Criseyde and to accompany her to her
father's tent. Enroute he swears to be her friend
and begs that she will treat him as a brother.

Days pass. For Troilus they are an anguish
"bitwixen hope and drede." He languishes and
waits, making a song which "with softe vois" he
sings for his beloved.

Just here in the story Chaucer describes her.

Criseyde mene was of hire stature,
Therto of shap, of face, and ek of cheere,
Ther myghte ben no fairer creature.
And ofte tyme this was hire manere,
To gon ytressed with hire heres clere
Doun by hire coler at hire bak byhynde,
Which with a thred of gold she wolde bynde.

And, save hire browes joyneden yfere,
Ther nas no lak, in aught I kan espien.
But for to speken of hire eyen cleere,
Lo, trewely, they writen that hire syen,

That Paradis stood formed in hire yen.
And with hire riche beaute evere more
Strof love in hire ay, which of hem was more.

She sobre was, ek symple, and wys withal,
The best ynorisshed ek that myghte be,
And goodly of hire speche in general,
Charitable, estatlich, lusty, and fre;
Ne nevere mo ne lakked hire pite;
Tendre-herted, slydynge of corage;
But trewely, I kan nat telle hire age.

The "slydynge" courage of Criseyde is the single but the overwhelming flaw in her perfections. Against the background of her quisling father and her carrion-minded uncle, she had worse than no precedent for fidelity.

On the tenth day after her leaving Troy, Diomede is at her father's tent, "fressh as braunche in May." The inevitable follows with treacherous speed. He takes her glove. She gives him among other things—"and that was litel nede"—the brooch that had belonged to Troilus. And Chaucer adds briefly: "Men seyn—I not—that she yaf hym hire herte."

Her perfidy had upon it all the marks of a mortal betrayal: a grave matter, reflection, full consent of will. All these she implies in her confession which is crassly innocent of any form of contrition.

She seyde, "Allas! for now is clene ago
My name of trouthe in love, for everemo!
For I have falsed oon the gentileste
That evere was, and oon the worthieste!

"Allas! of me, unto the worldes ende,
Shal neyther ben ywriten nor ysonge
No good word, for thise bokes wol me shende.
O, rolled shal I ben on many a tonge!
Throughout the world my belle shal be ronge!
And wommen moost wol haten me of alle.
Allas, that swich a cas me sholde falle!"

A letter, stained with tears, from Troilus she answers with cool nonchalance. She may return to him, she says, but in what year or day she does not know. Meanwhile and to her life's end he may regard her as a friend. By degrees, Troilus realizes

"That al is lost that he hath ben aboute."

Proof comes to hand with pitiless rapidity. Spoils of battle are brought into the city, among

them a coat of Diomede's. On the collar of it
Troilus finds

A broche, that he Criseyde yaf that morwe
That she from Troie moste nedes twynne,
In remembraunce of hym and of his sorwe.
And she hym leyde ayeyn hire feith to borwe
To kepe it ay! But now ful wel he wiste,
His lady nas no lenger on to triste.

If knighthood ever had its flowering it comes
to full and perfect blossom here; not in the rap-
ture of reciprocated love but in the bitterness of
its betrayal. Troilus asks with all the courtliness of
the perfect, gentle knight

"O lady myn, Criseyde,
Where is youre feith, and where is youre biheste?
Where is youre love? where is youre trouthe?"

. . .

"Was ther non other broche yow liste lete
To feffe with youre newe love," quod he,
"But thilke broch that I, with teris wete,
Yow yaf, as for a remembraunce of me?"

Beyond the pain of his bewildered disillusionment, he has no word of bitterness and no reproach for her. Faithful as she is false, he makes
this brave renewal of fidelity:

"That yow, that doon me al this wo endure,
Yet love I best of any creature!"

Parenthetically, two hundred years later Shakespeare, too, rises past the point of blame to this defense of women which he puts upon the lips of Troilus:

"Let it not be believed for womanhood.
Think we had mothers."

The story moves quickly to its end. Diomede is slain in battle. Troilus is killed in combat. Calkas, Pandarus, Criseyde, the faithless three, remain, a dubious argument for the survival of the fittest. Humanly, there is nothing more to say. And so Chaucer concludes the narrative with the behest:

"Go, litel bok, go, litel myn tragedye,
Ther God thi makere yet, er that he dye,
So sende myght to make in som comedye!
But litel book, no makyng thow n'envie,
But subgit be to alle poesye;
And kis the steppes, where as thow seest pace
Virgile, Ovide, Omer, Lucan, and Stace."

Then comes the sequel, brief, unmistakable, climactic, a complete and sublimated fulfillment of poetic justice.

Troilus has been slain. Immediately his soul

ascends to the eighth circle of the Ptolemaic heavens, leaving behind all the material elements, earth, air, fire, water, proper to the science of that day. From the circle of the fixed stars, he sees the order of the heavens and listens to the ravishing music of their harmony. From this celestial height he looks down on

"This litel spot of erthe, that with the se
Embraced is."

He cannot but despise the wretchedness of the world and all its vanities when compared with the full felicity of heaven.

In his beatitude he laughs celestially at those on earth who are weeping for his death. He condemns the blind desires of a world that cannot last, for now he knows that all our hearts must find their home in heaven.

This, Chaucer says, is for Troilus, the end of love, this the reward of his great worthiness, this all his bliss. Ended, too, is the false and brittle world. In this climax ascending Troilus is uplifted to his place in heaven, out of the tragedy that came of his loving Criseyde.

The story is perennial. Set in a classic pagan, if not a legendary past, environed with the repetitious and amorous technics of courtly love, the mereness of its humanity, the simplicity of its

tragedy can easily be blurred. Its ethics and morality are wholly within the cult of Venus. An
exposition of that cult is beside the purpose here.
Dante christianizes and sanctifies its idealization
of womanhood in his *Divine Comedy*. This is perhaps the best of all commentaries on this elaborate
system as it affected medieval life and thought.

Its impact upon a Christian civilization, upon
his own time, upon the youth to whom the story
must inevitably make its most direct appeal, Chaucer never lost sight of. His invective against the
sheer paganism of the setting comes within the
last twenty lines of the book:

Lo here, of payens corsed olde rites,
Lo here, what alle hire goddes may availle;
Lo here, thise wrecched worldes appetites;

His definition of moral emphasis is equally
clear. Indeed it would be hard to find in literature a more unambiguous statement of purpose,
nor a more exalted one. This is his great address to
youth.

O yonge, fresshe folkes, he or she,
In which that love up groweth with youre age,
Repeyreth hom fro worldly vanyte,
And of youre herte up casteth the visage
To thilke God that after his ymage

Yow made, and thynketh al nys but a faire
This world, that passeth soone as floures faire.

And loveth hym, the which that right for love
Upon a crois, oure soules for to beye,
First starf, and roos, and sit in hevene above;
For he nyl falsen no wight, dar I seye,
That wol his herte al holly on hym leye.
And syn he best to love is, and most meke,
What nedeth feynede loves for to seke?

If a writer ever clarifies his objectives and position it is at the end of his work. Chaucer has
done this unmistakably. Robinson, commenting
on this says: "When Chaucer has followed the
tragic story to the end his closing comment is not,
like Boccaccio's, a mere condemnation of faithless women; nor is it strictly a reprobation of the
special ethics of courtly love. It is a Christian
counsel to fix the heart upon the unfailing love
of God. The earnestness of the appeal and the
elevation of its mood leave no doubt of Chaucer's
essentially religious spirit."

Here we are face to face with Chaucer, in the
richest years of his life, in the fullness of his de-
veloped genius. He has just completed his greatest
book; to speak in the idiom of our day, a super
book of the month and quite beyond the Pulitzer

novel of the year or of the centuries. Chaucer is not writing for these, for royalties, for film or radio rights. He has concluded his tragedy swiftly and directly with but a backward glance at Criseyde. He has translated Troilus to the heavens of Dante as well as of Ptolemy. He could have done no more for his beatification. This is his masterpiece, his "supreme example of sustained narrative." He is probably not aware of that, certainly not pre-occupied with the thought. He has a dearer concern, one which almost describes him with a new nobility and a beautifully focussed care. He is intent upon the boys and girls of his own day, the only ones that he could have guessed would read his "litel boke." Troilus and Criseyde were young and brave and beautiful. His story is a tragedy of youth as is also its catharsis. The happy ending so yearned for by the human heart, and most of all by youth, must always be the supernatural one. That is what he tells these fourteenth century boys and girls.

His thought no doubt moves back to all who will read his book but especially to the "yonge fresshe folkes," and all the ardours of their youth. He is solicitous for them. He knows the vicarious experiences of love that they seek in the tales of old romance. He asks them, as a father might, not to seek these fictitious and feigned loves. Christ crucified for them, Christ risen from that death is their love as He is their redeemer. Youth has seldom been more honored than by Chaucer's great address to them.

First Things and Last

First Things and Last

MORE than a thousand years ago the wise West Saxon King Alfred translated into the English of his time one of the most widely known of all books in the Latin tongue, *De Consolatione Philosophiae* of Boethius. It was for himself and his people what Gregory's *Pastoral Care* was for his priests. On it he hung his own commentaries on kingship, for instance; one qualification being that a king should wear a beard. From it he drew metaphysical and ethical notions of time and eternity and their relations. From it the Beowulf scribe may have found articulate the spirit of his gnomic passages. However that may be, the *Consolation of Philosophy* summarized, formed and informed the philosophic thought of the England of Alfred.

More than a hundred years before Columbus and his crew planted the Holy Cross on the island of San Salvador, the Controller of Customs, Geoffrey Chaucer, in his house above Aldgate, translated into the English of his day from his Latin and French texts that outstanding epitome of philosophic thought of the Europe of his day, Boethius' *Consolation of Philosophy*. Into it he interjected a minimum of himself. From it he drew epithet, theory and theme for anything from a line to an entire poem. Boethius inhabited his work. He pervaded contemporary thought. In a world that had changed all things from its tongue to its throne, Boethius remained unchanged.

Two hundred years later with the keen scholarship that was hers, the learned Queen Elizabeth translated into an English that is ours the *Consolation of Philosophy*. She was bent upon the specific exercise of "Englishing" and her translation is accordingly faithful. An England undreamed by Alfred, unguessed by Chaucer she governed and yet a thousand years had been a day in the matter of philosophic fundamental thought, and that thought was still best epitomized in Boethius. He was the spokesman of the three great periods of English literature, if we wish so to divide it: the Old, the Middle, the Modern; or in terms of dominating personalities: the ages of Alfred, of Chaucer, of Elizabeth. He has been translated repeatedly since. A book that stands by so deliberate a choice at the great cross roads of English life and thought must have some genuine claim to consideration. It has.

The *Consolation of Philosophy* is one of the great central or pivotal books of the world. It is the meeting place of the ancient, medieval, and modern worlds in point of time; of pagan and

Christian worlds in point of creed. It is not original but a summary of what philosophy has to offer to a man in the last extremities of life, a man in prison and condemned to death. It seeks truth not as a quest but as a moral support. It is uncontroversial, neo-platonic, not committed to any doctrine, reducing its terms to the lowest common denominator of all civilized philosophies and religions. For all these reasons it turns out to be the most universal as well as the most interesting example of prison literature the world has ever seen. Dante, at the death of Beatrice set himself "to read that book of Boethius . . . wherein, when a prisoner and an exile, he had found consolation." Milton puts the speech of Boethius on the lips of Lycidas and Samson. And although his philosophy, as a system, passed into total eclipse behind the shadow cast by the scientific age, his idiom is still on the lips of Tennyson, and indeed, his way to Beatitude has never been abandoned by those who seek Truth not in matter only but in Spirit.

It is a book written under the extremities of Job and the sentence of Socrates, with the faith of one and the reason of the other. Boethius had been born into consular rank in Rome about 470 or 480. As a friend of the Ostrogothic ruler Theodoric he enjoyed prestige. As a profound student of Greek language and philosophy he enjoyed even as a young man the reputation for great learning. Falsely accused of treason, magic, and sacrilege he was exiled and imprisoned in Pavia where, in 524 or 525, he was brutally put to death. The remorse and repentance of Theodoric came too late to save him.

The sentence executed upon the life of his body left his great apology untouched. It survives as a text on philosophic orthodoxy of his day. Down through the centuries it came with the epics of Thebes and Troy, with the deeds of the Romans, the dream of Scipio, the metamorphoses of Ovid, the commentaries of Cicero and Macrobius and Saint Jerome. Into Chaucer's world of books it inevitably found its way where it became the treatise "which most profoundly influenced his thought . . . and on which he drew throughout his life."[1]

His philosophic digressions in the *Troilus* and the *Knight's Tale* confess his inability to resist the wisdom of his master, even under the impact of his own mature creative gifts. His *"Wordes Unto Adam, His Owne Scriveyn"* indicate something of the solicitude with which he regarded his translation of Boethius.

This translation of the *Consolation of Philos-*

[1] J. L. Lowes' *Geoffrey Chaucer*, p. 90.

ophy he made probably about 1380. The work adds not a cubit to his stature for either prose or verse. The prose throughout is mediocre. The verses which in the original alternate with the prose treatises through five short books he did not trouble to transpose into English verse. Using a French translation beside his heavily glossed Latin original he probably was much more concerned with literal accuracy than with literary excellence. That he did not achieve both need not be imputed against him.

For us the important thing about his *Boece,* as he calls it, is that it provides the succinct and established picture of his philosophic world, the map on which his theological bearings are all marked. Through the eyes of Boethius he looks out upon all existence, its first cause, its last end, the universe, the world, God, man.

The universe he sees as a wheel that bears the stars, made by God and fastened to the fixed chair, which is His throne. God turns these heavens with a ravishing sway, producing night and day, the seasons, the winds, the music of the spheres. He rules them by His laws and holds them all in place by love. The earth is a prick in this universe, one-fourth of it being habitable. Man lives in the least prick of this prick, "this wyde world which that men seye is round."

The world in time and as distinct from the earth is the floor of double-visaged Fortune, a personification or allegory for change. All conditions of life are hers. She distributes them blindly; the figure of her activity is the turning of the wheel. Her gifts or withdrawals have no connection with the deserts of men. God uses them as a discipline.

The world under the aspect of eternity is created freely by God and governed by His love and reason for its perfect end. All nature takes those causes from the stability of His divine thought. If laws ceased discord would immediately result.

God, the first cause, the unmoved Mover is eternal, omniscient, omnipotent, sovereign-good and happiness. Because He is man's Maker, man should have pride in such ancestry. The universe itself is proof of the existence of God. The difference between the dispensations of God and of Fortune would not confuse men if they knew all the reasons for all things.

The nature of evil, Boethius says, metaphysically speaking, is nothing. All being is good. All things that are not good fail in that degree to be. All men that are not good fail to possess God and are turned to beasts. Sin is the malady of soul through which this comes to pass.

Man is a divine beast, a citizen of God's country,

possessed of four passions and a triple soul. He is a reasonable two-footed beast who in his dignity among animals walks upright. His five wits or senses and his imagination or power to form images he shares with other animals. His reason by which he apprehends universals and his immortality are proper to man alone.

These, the first things and the last for Boethius are first and last for Chaucer also. The thousand years that separated them in time did nothing to separate them in the great realms of truth nor to touch the orthodox Christianity of their theology, their philosophy, their metaphysics. Across the centuries the contemporary reader can share with them these great freedoms of Christian philosophy. The Boethian intimations from Plato, his reconditioning of pagan myths, his elaborations on Aristotelian psychology and ethics all floodlight the later narratives of Chaucer and reveal the philosophic ground on which in his maturity he came to rest.

The *Consolation of Philosophy* is obviously basic to any adequate understanding of Chaucer. None but the research student will read in the Latin this work of applied philosophy, nor Chaucer's translation. For this reason a summary of it will probably not be gratuitous. In this day of digests it may be quite in order.

The treatise is written in five books, each comprised of alternating poems and short prose essays. As has already been said, Chaucer paraphrases the poems, not troubling to put them into verse form. Considering his copious metrical translations, to mention *The Romaunt of the Rose* as one case for all, one can only conclude that his prime concern here is with philosophy.

In the first book Wisdom appears as a woman to Boethius in prison to console him. Representing both the active and the contemplative life she reproves the Muses who cannot truly comfort man and assures Boethius from examples of the great Greeks that philosophy never deserts the innocent. Virtue is man's security. Wisdom cooperates with God to help those in need, of whom she cites contemporary examples. To the tumult in the mind of Boethius over existing evil, his own virtuous life and its ironic end, the ordered beauty in nature and the disordered world of men, Wisdom states in a Job-like dialogue that there is a proper season for all things, that God made the world and governs it, and that man cannot be exiled from the city of his choice. Hope is his security in time. Discussion rises gradually from the pagan allegory of Plato through the metaphysics of Aristotle, to the Christianity of Saint Paul and Saint Augustine.

The second book presents **Fortune**, two-faced and blind, her caprices and her apology. She acts according to her nature which is change. In taking goods from man she deprives him of nothing that belongs to him. Plenty does not relieve wretchedness but makes men covetous. A catalog of the past blessings of Boethius stands in contrast to those that remain. Man wrongs God by seeking other than his proper good. This he finds in self-knowledge, in his own nobility over all creation which results in both perfect freedom and perfect detachment. Power is a mockery, "a mows against other mys". Neither it nor any of the gifts of Fortune are to be desired because they are not always possessed by good men, nor does their possession make men good. The smallness of earth, the emptiness of glory stand in sharp contrast to the happiness of heaven. Capricious and unfaithful Fortune leaves man only his friends. Love that rules the universe must rule the heart of man.

Throughout the third book Boethius meets Philosophy in Platonic dialogue considering the catharsis wrought by evil Fortune, the universal quest for happiness and its ultimate being in God. Happiness is not found in riches, dignity, power, glory nor in any physical thing, but in God alone Who is sovereign good. God and happiness are one and as the perfect good are man's proper end.

In his fourth book Boethius moves into the world of metaphysics. He considers the intrinsic weakness of the wicked, the strength of the good who alone are free. Being is good and he who abandons good stops being. There is no proper place for hatred in the world. Sin is itself a malady of the soul. The circumstances under which the book was written give great pertinence to the fine discussion on fortune, prudence, destiny and the ways of God with men.

The *Consolation of Philosophy* rises to its strong inspiring climax in the fifth book. Here one meets immortal questions, the impossibility of chance, the possibility of prayer, the free will of man and its degrees, the foreknowledge of God which is necessary to His Being. Reason, being man's most excellent and peculiar faculty, teaches submission to God. The book concludes with the commendation with which Boethius met the human injustice of his death and the divine mercy of its reward.

> Withstond thanne and eschue thou vices; worschipe and love thou vertues; areise thi corage to ryghtful hopes; yilde thou humble preieres an heygh. Gret necessite of prowesse and vertu is encharged and comaunded to yow, yif ye nil nat dissimulen; syn that ye worken and don (that is to seyn, your dedes

or your werkes) byforn the eyen of the juge
that seeth and demeth alle thinges.

Here then is the apology of Boethius, those
first and last things in life for him, coming to us
in Chaucer's own current English. They bring us
to, and bring to us the great stabilities of existence, a world where a God of love and immortal
man were realities and powers beside which
atomic fission would have been a breath in the
wind. They come to us from a world in which
men's wills were free scientifically and experi-
mentally, from a world in which men were not
dissected; they were immortalized. One finds cold
comfort in the consolation of modern philosophy.
It is good to turn with Chaucer to the prison cell
in Pavia and there to cheer one's heart and mind
with the wisdom of Boethius.

GLOSSARY

Any one who can read the sports pages of an American newspaper should find Chaucer fairly easy. The present arbitrary state of spelling obviates still further difficulties in the reading of Middle English.

The following partial glossary provides definitions for words in the texts quoted in these essays, the meanings of which are not immediately apparent. They are given here in the same grammatical forms in which they occur in the texts.

A

Al-day, at any time
Amonesteth, admonishes
Ancille, servant
Areise, exalt
Arrette, attribute
Assyse, judgment
Axe, Axeth, ask
Ayein, again

B

Bak, back
Beede, offer
Behovely, proper
Bihoven, belong
Bobaunce, boast
Brennynge, burnings
Byforn, before

C

Ches, chose
Cleped, named
Coler, neck
Convenable, convenient
Coppe, cup
Corage, mind, will
Coveyteth, desires

Creaunce, credit
Crois, cross

D

Debonayre, gracious
Deed, dead
Defaute, defect
Demeth, judges
Desport, mirth
Destreyneth, requires
Digne, worthy
Dissimulen, dissemble
Don, do
Doute, doubt
Dyvyne, divine

E

Eft-soone, very soon
Egre, keen
Ellys, else
Engyn, skill
Entame, open
Enjoynen, impose
Eschue, avoid
Eyen, eyes

F

Fayle, fail

Feffe, to endow
Ferthing, drop
Fetisly, gracefully
Feynede, false
Fille, fell
Flawmes, flames
Foo, foe
Forlete, forsake
Forleteth, abandons
Fyngres, fingers

G

Gabbere, liar
Gauded, adorned
Gilt, guilt
Gost, spirit, soul
Grece, grease

H

Haleth, draw
Halt, keeps
Han, have
Hele, health
Heyghe, high
Hoot, fervent

J

Japere, jester
Juge, judge

K

Koude, could

L

Largesse, bounty
Leche, physician
Leden, lead
Leet, let
Lete, yield

Liste, pleased, wished

M

Medled, mixed
Mene, medium, mediator
Mete, meat, meals
Misericorde, mercy
Mochel, much
Mows, mouse
Moo, more
Mys, mice
Mysdoon, done amiss

N

Namore, never more
Narwe, close
Nil nat, will not

O

Omelies, homilies
Onys, once
Orizonte, horizon
Over-lippe, upper lip

P

Perisse, perish
Peyned, took pains
Pighte, pierced
Pleyn, full
Pleynynge, lament
Preieres, prayers
Privee, private
Pyneth, repines

R

Refut, refuge
Renne, run
Reuthe, pity
Rial, royal

S

Seeche, seek
Semyly, Semely, becoming
Sheene, bright
Shende, reproach
Shrift, confession
Shrive, confess
Siker, certain
Sikerly, surely
Sikernesse, security
Sith, since
Sleen, slay
Slydynge, unstable
Smoot, struck
Sorwe, Sorweth, sorrow, sorrows
Sownen, tend toward
Spak, spoke
Spilt, spoiled
Starf, died
Stinte, Stynte, discontinue
Swich, such
Syen, saw

T

Targe, shield
Teene, grief
Thilke, such, this
Thurgh, through
Tobreste, burst
Tretys, well-formed
Trowe, believe
Tweye, two
Twyes, twice

U

Unkonnynge, ignorance
Unnethe, with difficulty
Unwemmed, spotless

W

Wastel-breed, fine, white bread
Waymentynge, lament
Weel, well
Wende, supposed
Wepen, weapon
Werre, trouble
Weyes, ways
Wight, person
Wikke, wicked
Wisse, instruct
Withstond, withstand
Wole, will
Woninge, dwelling
Woot, Wot, knows
Worchynge, working
Wratthe, offend
Wurthi, worthy
Wympul, white collar and head piece of a nun's dress
Wyped, wiped
Wyten, know

Y

Yaf, gave
Yen, eyes
Yerde, stick
Yeven, given
Yfere, together
Yilde, submit
Ysee, see, behold
Ytressed, with hair braided